Melody of Shiva Panchakshari

Story of Anaya

Rutvik Dharme

Instagram : @maha_shiva_

2ⁿᵈ Edition

ILLUSTRATIONS BY

ARAVIND KUMAR NALAWADE

@andy8_arts

Contents

Introduction

Chapter 1 : Infinite God Śiva

Chapter 2 : Selfless Devotion

Chapter 3 : Divine Gift by Śiva

Chapter 4 : Magic of Flute

Chapter 5 : Śiva Pañcākṣarī

Chapter 6 : Greatness of Holy Name

Chapter 7 : Bhasma and Rudrākṣa

Chapter 8 : Nīlakaṇṭha Rudra

Chapter 9 : Śiva the Saviour

Chapter 10 : Śiva's Supreme Mercy

I dedicate this book
to Paramaśiva and
Parāśakti

அலைமலிந்த புனல்மங்கை
ஆணாயர்க் அடியேன்

I bow in devotion to Anaya Nayanar as his servant's servant, whose divine music became a means to attain Moksha

Sundarmurthi Nayanar

वक्रतुण्ड महाकाय सूर्यकोटि समप्रभ।

निर्विघ्नं कुरु मे देव सर्वकार्येषु सर्वदा॥

O Lord Gaṇeśa, with a curved trunk and
mighty body, whose splendour equals a
million suns, please remove all obstacles from
all my undertakings, always.

गुरुर्ब्रह्मा गुरुर्विष्णुः गुरुर्देवो महेश्वरः ।

गुरुः साक्षात् परं ब्रह्म तस्मै श्रीगुरवे नमः ॥

The Guru is Brahmā, the Guru is Viṣṇu, the
Guru is Lord Maheśvara (Śiva); the Guru is
truly the Supreme Absolute, to that revered
Guru, I bow in reverence.

सरस्वति नमस्तुभ्यं वरदे कामरूपिणि।

विद्यारम्भं करिष्यामि सिद्धिर्भवतु मे सदा॥

O Goddess Sarasvatī, bestower of boons and embodiment of desire's form, I bow to You as I begin my pursuit of knowledge; may success be mine always.

Introduction

I bow down to Śrī Vighneśvara, the elephant-headed God and the remover of obstacles, who blesses the beginning of every sacred piece of work. May he grant a clear path and undisturbed focus to this humble effort. I offer my salutations to Devī Pārvatī and Śrī Parameśvara the eternal Lord of Lords who is both the protector and the Supreme Guru of all beings. My reverence also extends to Skanda the mighty commander of the celestial forces, born of Śiva's divine spark. May Bhagavān Śiva the all-pervading Omniscient Lord shower his grace upon me, so that I may glorify him through this offering of devotion. I dedicate this work to the one who performs the cosmic dance in the golden hall of Tillai, Śrī Naṭarāja of Citambaram. In that mystic space, he dances the rhythm of creation, preservation, and dissolution. It is in this divine rhythm that the Melody of Pañcākṣarī resounds eternally the sacred mantra "Namaḥ Śivāya", echoing through every atom of the cosmos. This book is an offering and a garland of words strung with devotion to that Eternal Dancer the Lord of Consciousness. This humble work narrates the inspiring and transformative tale of Āṇāya Nāyaṉār, one of the illustrious 63 Nāyaṉmārs the great Śaiva saints of Tamil Nadu whose lives were immersed in devotion. Āṇāya a wandering cowherd held no scholarly knowledge nor Vedic learning, yet his heart overflowed with innocent and ego-less love for Bhagavān Śiva. With nothing, but his flute and unwavering faith, he sang the Pañcākṣarī mantra with such intensity that even wild animals paused to listen, and the Lord himself was drawn by its melody. The purpose of this book is to dive deep into the life, devotion, and spiritual journey of Āṇāya Nāyaṉār, not merely as a historical account, but as a living flame that can ignite true devotion within the reader. Through his story, we also explore the supreme importance of the Pañcākṣarī mantra "Namaḥ Śivāya", which is praised in the Śrutis as the very heart of the Vedas. It is not just a mantra; it is the essence of dharma, the bridge to liberation, and the call of the soul toward the Infinite.

The Deity of Pañcākṣarī mantra is none other than Śrī Śiva himself, the embodiment of compassion, wisdom, and transcendence. This book shines light upon the greatness of his holy name, the purifying power of Bhasma (sacred ash), and the sanctity of Rudrākṣa, which adorns the body of the Lord and the hearts of his devotees. The symbolism and spiritual depth behind these sacred elements are discussed, so that all may grasp their essence. Moreover, this book includes tales that glorify Śrī Śiva as Nīlakaṇṭha the one who drank the deadly poison for the welfare of all beings. These stories reveal his boundless mercy, willingness to suffer for others, and the supreme ideal of Karuṇā (compassion). Whether appearing as a fiery pillar beyond comprehension, or as a mendicant moving among the poor, Śiva remains the Supreme Lord (Parameśvara) accessible to those with a pure and humble heart. Through the divine melody of devotion, this book seeks to awaken in the reader a longing for the Lord, an understanding of the beauty of surrender, and the realization that it is not ritual nor scholarship that moves the Divine, but pure and ego-less love. Let this work serve as a humble Nāda-pūjā a musical offering of words and devotion at the feet of Śrī Śiva. Let the sacred syllables of "Namaḥ Śivāya" ring through these pages like awakening, calling every heart back to its true source Śiva the unborn, undying, and ever-compassionate Lord of all.

Chapter 1

Infinite God Śiva

In the sacred Ekākṣara Upaniṣad, the very first verse offers a profound and beautiful description of Śrī Śiva, revealing his true nature as the Supreme Reality. The verse says **"You are the Imperishable (Akṣaraṁ), the one who is always accompanied by Umā (Pārvatī). You are known through the path of Suṣumnā Nāḍī. You are firm Principle. You are the unmoving, eternal principle (Sthāṇuḥ) and ancient source of this world. You are the essence of Praṇava (Om). You are the very principle of life-giving water. You are the protector and saviour of the universe."** (Ekakshara Upanishad Verse 1)

Each of these descriptions is filled with spiritual truth and deep symbolism. Let us understand this verse and its connection with the Upaniṣads and Vedas in detail.

Śiva as Akṣara - The Imperishable

The word Akṣara in Sanskrit means that which is imperishable, unchanging, and beyond destruction. In the Vedas, this word is used to describe Brahman, the Supreme Reality the eternal principle behind all creation. That same Brahman is called Śiva in many scriptures. Śiva in his highest form is beyond all. He was never born and will never die.

The Kena Upaniṣad one of the principal Upaniṣads directly hints at this. It speaks about the Supreme Brahman which cannot be grasped by the mind, eyes, or senses, and then Umā Haimavatī the goddess Umā explains this highest Brahman to the gods. Umā is always seen beside Śiva. So, the seers understood that the one who is always with Umā is Śiva and he is Brahman.

Śiva with Umā - The Lord and his Power

The Ekākṣara Upaniṣad clearly says, "You are the one accompanied by Umā." In Vedic and Purāṇic understanding, Śiva and Śakti (Umā) are not two separate beings. They are two aspects of one Supreme Reality. Just like heat cannot be separated from fire, Śakti (energy) cannot be separated from Śiva (consciousness). The creation, maintenance, and destruction of the universe are all possible only because of this divine union of Śiva and Śakti. Śakti is the power of Śiva. In the Puruṣa Sūkta and other Vedic hymns, it is explained that the creation emerges from

Puruṣa. That Puruṣa is Śiva, and his energy that expresses as nature and creation is Prakṛti or Śakti. Thus, Śiva is the doer, and Śakti is his doing. He is always with Umā, Pārvatī, or Śakti because they are truly inseparable.

The Suṣumnā Nāḍī - The Inner Path

The Upaniṣad also says "You are known through the path of Suṣumnā." In yogic understanding, the Suṣumnā Nāḍī is the central spiritual channel in the human subtle body. It runs through the spine and is activated through meditation and Prāṇāyāma. When the Kuṇḍalinī Śakti rises through the Suṣumnā, the seeker experiences the presence of Śiva within as pure consciousness beyond thought. So, Śiva is not just some being in the Śivaloka or Kailāśa. He is the inner Self, the Atman, realized through deep meditation, especially through the path of Suṣumnā.

Śiva as Sthāṇu - The Immovable

Śiva is called by the name Sthāṇu, meaning unmoving, steady, and fixed. In contrast to the ever-changing world, Śiva represents that which does not change. He is the eternal principle behind the dance of creation and destruction. Śivaliṅga the most worshipped symbol of Śiva represents this formless, infinite reality. It has no beginning, no end. It is not a person with limbs, but a symbol of limitless Brahman. This is why the formless aspect of God, or nirguṇa Brahman, is worshipped as Śiva in the form of the Liṅga.

Śiva as the Water of Life

The Upaniṣad also describes Śiva as the very form of life-giving water. Just as water is essential for all life, Śiva is the inner essence of all beings. All life arises from him, is sustained by him, and dissolves back into him. Without Śiva, there is no life. Even Ganga the sacred river flows from the matted locks of Śiva. This symbolically shows that all purity, nourishment, and life force originates from him.

Śiva as Loka Rakṣakaḥ

Lastly, the Upaniṣad says, "You are the protector and saviour of the worlds." Śiva is not only the transcendental Brahman but also Īśvara, the one who protects the universe. He took the form of Nīlakaṇṭha to drink the Hālāhala poison during the ocean churning, to save all beings. He is Mrityuñjaya, the conqueror of death, who saves devotees from fear, sorrow, and rebirth. When he takes a form to act in the world, he is called Saguna Brahman God with qualities or Mahādeva, Īśvara, Bhagavān. But even then, he remains Akṣara unchanging at the core.

Śiva as Brahman - The Supreme Truth of the Vedas

According to the Vedas, the Supreme Truth is Brahman the formless, infinite, eternal principle. But the same Vedas give this Brahman a name Śiva. The Yajurveda mentions Śiva as the highest. The Atharvaśiras Upaniṣad clearly declares that Śiva is Brahman, Śiva is Īśvara, Śiva is all. The Kaivalya Upaniṣad says "Śiva is alone, without attributes, and without duality. In the Vedic vision, Brahman and Śiva are not different. When we say Brahman, we refer to the highest truth and that truth, the Upaniṣads reveal is Śiva. Śiva as both

Formless and Formed. The Upaniṣadic sages clearly described two aspects of this one Supreme Being.

1. **Nirguṇa Śiva** - The formless, beyond qualities, infinite. This is Brahman, represented by the Śiva Liṅga, meditated upon in deep silence.

2. **Saguṇa Śiva** - The one who takes form out of compassion for the world. This is Mahādeva, with Goddess Umā beside him, adorned with crescent moon, Ganga, tiger skin, and Rudrākṣa.

These are the two aspects of one Supreme Śiva.

Creation as the Energy of Śiva

In the Vedic texts, it is said that Brahman alone existed in the beginning. Then,

Brahman became two Puruṣa (Consciousness) and Prakṛti (Nature).

Puruṣa is Śiva - The witness, the unmoving, the eternal.

Prakṛti is Śakti - The creative force, Goddess Umā.

All the universe is born from this union. The Gītā, Sāṁkhya, and Upaniṣads agree on this truth. Thus, creation is not separate from Śiva, it is his play through Śakti. The Vedas say that only a quarter of Śiva becomes creation and the rest remains beyond, in divine transcendence. This idea appears in the Puruṣa Sūkta, which says "One-quarter of him becomes the world, three-quarters remain unknown above."

The Ekākṣara Upaniṣad, though brief, captures the highest truths of the Vedas.

Śiva is Brahman, the imperishable truth.

He is both without form and with form.

He is the inner self, known through Suṣumnā.

He is the life-force, the protector, and the eternal principle.

With Umā, he is complete. Without her, he does not create or act.

To know Śiva is to know Brahman. To surrender to Śiva is to reach the highest spiritual realization.

Śiva - The Supreme Divine

Beyond this visible world of names and forms, beyond the cycles of time and change, beyond even the highest knowledge of the Vedas there exists a reality so vast, so luminous, that even the scriptures can only hint at it. This is the Supreme Reality, the Ultimate Truth, who is called by sages and saints as Bhagavān Śiva. The Vedas the most ancient spiritual texts of India declare Brahman to be imperishable, infinite, and all-pervading. But even the Vedas admit their limitation that they can reveal only a portion of that Supreme Reality. Only a quarter of the Divine is manifest in creation. The remaining three quarters are entirely beyond material existence, beyond even the grasp of Vedic rituals and words. That infinite, unmanifest part is not even known to the Vedas.

The Merciful Descent of Śiva

Though he is formless, beyond attributes, and untouched by time or space, Śiva is also infinitely compassionate. Out of love for his devotees, He assumes a form, a blissful and divine appearance, so that the human mind can hold on to him in meditation and worship. This form is not ordinary. It is luminous, serene, and filled with divine grace. By meditating upon this beautiful form of Śiva adorned with crescent moon, sacred ash, matted locks, and Rudrākṣa beads. The devotee gradually moves inward, crossing the boundaries of thought and emotion, and reaches the state of samādhi. This form is a bridge to the formless. He is the bestower of well-being (śiva), the one whose very name means auspiciousness. By meditating on Śiva, one moves from the lower nature of the self to the higher, and finally reaches the liberated state of oneness.

Suṣumnā Nāḍī - Inner Path to Liberation

In the ancient science of yoga, the human body is seen not just as a physical structure but as an energetic system, filled with subtle channels called Nāḍīs. Among thousands of such energy channels, three Nāḍīs are considered the most important. They are Iḍā, Piṅgalā, and Suṣumnā. Iḍā Nāḍī starts on the left side of the body and is associated with the moon and cooling energy. Piṅgalā Nāḍī starts on the right side and is associated with the sun and heating energy. But Suṣumnā Nāḍī, running through the center of the spinal column, is the main channel - the highway of spiritual ascent. Suṣumnā is also known as Merudaṇḍa or Brahmadaṇḍa, the spiritual spine or staff of Brahman. It extends from the Mūlādhāra Chakra at the base of the spine to the Sahasrāra Chakra at the crown of the head. This central pathway is the sacred path through which the Kuṇḍalinī Śakti, the divine feminine energy, ascends. When a practitioner practices deep dhyāna (meditation) on Śrī Śiva, the dormant energy at the base of the spine awakens and begins its ascent through the Suṣumnā. The Utimate goal of yogic practice is to unite Kuṇḍalinī Śakti with Śrī Śiva at the Sahasrāra Chakra. When this union occurs, the devotee transcends all duality and enters the state of Samādhi perfect absorption and attains Mokṣa (liberation).

Śiva Resides at the Sahasrāra Chakra

The Sahasrāra, or the thousand-petaled lotus, is the highest energy center in the body. It is located at the top of the head and is the seat of pure consciousness. It is here that Śiva the Supreme Self is believed to reside. While other nāḍīs are spread throughout the body and have multiple functions, only Suṣumnā Nāḍī reaches all the way to Sahasrāra. Thus, Suṣumnā is the royal path that leads the spiritual seeker directly to Śiva. According to the Ekākṣara Upaniṣad, and echoed in various Tantric and Yogic scriptures, it is through Suṣumnā Nāḍī that the divine can be truly realized. When one meditates deeply and awakens this nāḍī, all other senses and dualities dissolve, and the truth of "Śivoham" which means "I am Śiva" becomes a living reality. There is no one except Śiva, he manifested as Universe.

Supporting Roles of Idā and Piṅgalā

While Suṣumnā is the main channel of liberation, the other two nāḍīs Idā and Piṅgalā also play vital roles. These nāḍīs are intertwined around the Suṣumnā and represent the dual forces within creation. Idā symbolizes mind, calmness, and intuition. Piṅgalā symbolizes action, heat, and logic. They cross each other at various chakras and help balance the energies in the human body. They serve as assistants to Suṣumnā. Without the harmony of Idā and Piṅgalā, the awakening of Suṣumnā remains difficult. However, these nāḍīs do not reach the Sahasrāra. That final liberation, the union with Śiva is possible only through Suṣumnā.

Śiva, Viṣṇu, and Brahmā - Deities of the three major Nāḍīs in human body

According to the Sūta Saṁhitā a sacred section of the Skanda Mahāpurāṇa, each of the three major Nāḍīs is governed by a deity. Śiva is the deity of Suṣumnā. Viṣṇu is the deity of Idā. Brahmā is the deity of Piṅgalā.

This reflects the harmony among the Trimūrti, or the three cosmic functions.

Creation (Brahmā - Piṅgalā)

Preservation (Viṣṇu - Idā)

Dissolution / Liberation (Śiva - Suṣumnā)

But among these, Śiva, as the deity of Suṣumnā leads the soul to its highest goal. Suṣumnā is the royal road to enlightenment, the channel of grace, and the path to transcendence.

Śiva is known through Suṣumnā Nāḍī

Spiritual liberation is not a destination one reaches by outer travel. It is the inward journey from the restless mind to the still Self and Suṣumnā Nāḍī is the inner path that leads straight to the abode of Śiva. The Ekākṣara Upaniṣad, echoing the voice of countless saints and sages declares "You are to be known through the Suṣumnā path." That is why yogis say, "If you wish to meet the Supreme Śiva, do not look outside. Go inward. Purify the mind. Awaken the Suṣumnā. Rise through it, and there, in the thousand-petaled lotus, in eternal stillness and bliss, Śiva." In the sacred Sūta Saṁhitā verse number 02:11:37, there is a profound verse that gives us a glimpse into the inner meaning of the human subtle body and its divine connection with the supreme beings.

सुषुम्नायाः शिवो देव इडाया देवता हरिः ।

पिङ्गलाया विरिञ्चिः स्यात्सरस्वत्या वीराण्मुने ॥ ३७ ॥

suṣumnāyāḥ śivo deva iḍāyā devatā hariḥ ।
piṅgalāyā viriñciḥ syātsarasvatyā vīrāṇmune ॥ 37 ॥

"The god who denotes Sūṣumṇā is Śiva, the deity of Iḍā is Hari, the deity of Piṅgalā is

Brahmā and the deity of Sarasvatī nāḍī is Virāṭ, O Muni!" Sūta Saṁhitā (02:11:37)

This one verse holds the entire map of the inner spiritual system and shows how the deities we worship externally are not separate from our own being. They live within us as energies, guiding our journey towards liberation. In this chapter, we will understand the secret meaning of this verse, and how Śiva is the Supreme reality connected with the central channel Sūṣumṇā.

The Three Major Nāḍīs - Iḍā, Piṅgalā, and Sūṣumṇā

In yogic understanding, there are 72,000 subtle energy channels in the human body, called nāḍīs. Out of these, three are the most important.

Sūṣumṇā Nāḍī - The central channel, running from the base of the spine (mūlādhāra cakra) to the crown of the head (sahasrāra cakra). It is the path of spiritual awakening.

Iḍā Nāḍī - Flows along the left side of the spine, connected to the moon's energy, calming and cooling. It is linked to the **right nostril**.

Piṅgalā Nāḍī - Flows along the right side of the spine, connected to the sun's energy, activating and heating. It is linked to the **left nostril**.

Each of these nāḍīs represents a divine force:

Iḍā is Viṣṇu (Hari) - The preserver, bringing balance and nurturing.

Piṅgalā is Brahmā - The creator, representing activity and outward movement.

Sūṣumṇā is Śiva - The destroyer of ignorance, the awakener, and the supreme path to liberation.

The Mystery of Liṅgodbhava

There is a famous purāṇic story told in the Liṅgodbhava episode. Once, Brahmā and Viṣṇu were debating who among them was the greatest. Suddenly, a massive pillar of fire (Liṅga) appeared, stretching across the heavens and deep into the underworld. Śiva had manifested as this infinite pillar of fire to teach a divine truth that the origin of the universe is beyond the understanding of ego and duality. Brahmā took the form of a swan and went upward to find the top of the pillar, while Viṣṇu took the form of a white boar and went downward to find its base. But neither could find the beginning nor the end. This story is not just an ancient myth. It is a spiritual metaphor for our own inner energy system. Viṣṇu (Iḍā) going downward represents the air we inhale through the right nostril. It goes down to energize the body. Brahmā (Piṅgalā) going upward represents the exhalation through the left nostril, releasing energy outward. But Śiva (Sūṣumṇā) remains still, straight, and infinite like the pillar of fire. It connects us to the divine crown the Sahasrāra. This is the pathway of real awakening. This is why the Liṅgodbhava Mūrti shows Śiva emerging as a pillar of fire, with Brahmā and Viṣṇu on either side symbolizing Iḍā and Piṅgalā Nāḍīs. Neither can reach his ends because

Sūṣumṇā is the only path that leads to liberation.

Symbolism in Breathing

The breath we take is not just air, it is prāṇa, or life force. When we inhale through the right nostril, energy flows down the Iḍā nāḍī. When we exhale through the left nostril, energy travels up the Piṅgalā nāḍī. In day-to-day life, we keep alternating between Iḍā and Piṅgalā. This is the dual nature of life, active and passive, creation and preservation, heat and cold, masculine, and feminine. But to realize the Self, one must go beyond this duality. That is where Sūṣumṇā comes in the central channel through which kuṇḍalinī rises during deep spiritual practice. Śiva is Sūṣumṇā steady, central, and infinite.

Liṅgodbhava Mūrti is Carved in Stone

In temples, the Liṅgodbhava Mūrti is always carved in stone, not metal. Why? Because fire (Śiva) and metal are natural opposites. Fire melts metal, but stone can withstand fire and remain firm. This is symbolic. That is why Śiva, the pillar of fire, is depicted in stone, teaching us the importance of becoming firm and steady in our Sādhanā (practice).

Ekapāda Trimūrti - Śiva as Single Support

Another important icon of Śiva is the Ekapāda Trimūrti, where Brahmā and Viṣṇu are seen emerging from the sides of Śiva, and Śiva is shown standing with only one leg.

Śiva's single leg represents the Sūṣumṇā nāḍī, the central support.

Brahmā and Viṣṇu emerging from either side represent Piṅgalā and Iḍā.

Iḍā is placed on the right, and Piṅgalā on the left. This is an important detail seen in yoga and sculpture.

In this form, Brahmā and Viṣṇu are not fully separate; they emerge from Śiva, reminding us that the energies of creation and preservation are not independent. They arise from the infinite Śiva. Śiva is the source, the support, and the sustainer.

Tripāda Trimūrti - The Three-Legged Form

In the Tripāda Trimūrti, the symbolism is extended even further. Here, Śiva has one leg (Sūṣumṇā). Brahmā and Viṣṇu each have one leg, making it three legs in total. Hence the name Tripāda means three-footed. This represents that the Trimūrti Brahmā (creation), Viṣṇu (preservation), and Śiva (destruction/liberation) are not three separate gods but one being manifesting in three ways. Śiva is the central pillar, while Brahmā and Viṣṇu are expressions of his energies. This also connects back to Iḍā, Piṅgalā, and Sūṣumṇā the three flows of energy, but one root source.

Śiva - The Eternal Source and Liberator

Through these forms Liṅgodbhava, Ekapāda Trimūrti, and Tripāda Trimūrti we understand that Śiva is the Supreme Being, beyond time and space. He is Pāśupati, the Lord of all bound souls, and the liberator. He controls the Pañcamahābhūtas the five elements earth, water, fire, air, and space. He pervades the universe in his Aṣṭamūrti form

- the eightfold manifestation. He is the silent observer, the supreme intelligence, and the inner guru. Even in our body, Iḍā and Piṅgalā are helpful, but they are limited. They cannot take us to the highest goal. Only Sūṣumṇā, the path of Śiva, can take us to the sahasrāra, the thousand-petaled lotus at the crown of the head, where pure consciousness resides. This is why Śiva is worshipped as the Liṅga, meaning a symbol beyond form, for he is the fire that burns ignorance and reveals the eternal truth. Śiva is not only in the temples but also within you. Every breath you take, every movement of prāṇa, every step on the spiritual path all are possible because of his silent support. Iḍā and Piṅgalā will keep the cycle of duality going. But Sūṣumṇā, the Śiva nāḍī, is the straight road to mokṣa. To walk on that path, keep your mind pure, your heart devoted, and your body disciplined. Worship the Liṅga within, the fire of Śiva, and rise beyond ego and illusion. For Śiva is the Self infinite, unborn, and ever free.

Śrī Mātā Pārvatī sameta Śrī Parameśvara Mahādeva on Nandi

Chapter 2

Selfless Devotion

In the sacred land of Tamil Nadu, lived a humble cowherd named Āṉāya Nāyaṉār. He belonged to a simple community of people who were known for their steadfast faith in Mahādeva. Though they lived amidst cattle and clay, their hearts pulsed with the purest devotion to the Supreme Lord. Āṉāya was not born into wealth or royal lineage, but he was rich in the currency that mattered most to Bhagavān Śiva that is Bhakti, the unwavering love and devotion that seeks nothing in return. He was a child of the open fields, walking barefoot through dewy grasslands and thick forests, always surrounded by his beloved cows. These cows were not just animals to him; they were sacred beings and companions in his life of devotion. Every morning, as the sun cast its golden glow upon the earth, Āṉāya would rise before dawn. He would gently awaken his cows, calling out to each by name. His voice was soft and melodious, filled with warmth. After milking them with care and affection, he would churn curd and prepare ghee, all from the milk offered by his gentle companions. The milk he received was not treated as a commodity, but as a sacred gift from Bhagavān himself.

With utmost reverence, he would set aside the finest milk for Abhiṣekaṁ, the ritual bathing of Śivaliṅga at the local temple. Holding a simple clay pot filled with pure milk, Āṉāya would walk barefoot to the temple, humming softly under his breath the holy name of Śiva. Every step he took was a step towards divine service. At the temple, he would offer the milk with love. Sometimes he would serve ghee and curd too, handing them over to the priests for use in the daily rituals. He never asked for anything in return not blessings, not recognition. For him, service to Śiva and service to Śiva's devotees were the same. He believed wholeheartedly that Mahādeva resides in those who worship him, and helping such devotees was no less than serving the Lord himself. Though many around him were focused on trade, wealth, or daily struggles, Aṇāya's life was steeped in a different kind of wealth. The wealth of selfless actions, sacred routines, and inner silence. He did not memorize complex scriptures or debate the meanings of Ślokas. His faith was simple, pure, and radiant like the flame of a temple lamp untouched by the wind. He believed that all forms of worship like chanting Stotras, singing Hymns, reciting Mantras must arise from a pure and ego-less heart. "What use is ritual without purity of heart?" he often said. "Śiva does not dwell in offerings made with pride or calculation. He lives in a simple heart that longs for him without motive."

One day, as he led his cows through a forest path, letting them graze beneath the shade of trees, his eyes caught sight of something unusual. He saw a great Sage seated beneath a spreading banyan tree. The ascetic's form was both serene and powerful. His body was smeared with Vibhūti sacred ash that covered his arms, chest, and forehead. His jata, matted locks, cascaded over his shoulders, and he sat in deep meditation with eyes closed. The entire atmosphere around the sage seemed charged with spiritual energy. A silent calm prevailed. Even the birds did not chirp too loudly, as if aware of the sanctity of the moment. Ānāya drawn by the radiance of the sage, approached quietly, and stood with folded hands. He waited with reverence until the sage's trance began to fade. Slowly, the great saint opened his eyes. The moment their eyes met, a silent recognition occurred. The Sage saw in Ānāya the fire of devotion, the innocence of a child, and the unshakable surrender of a true seeker. With a gentle voice, the sage spoke, "O child of Śiva, your love for him shines brighter than gold. You are already on the path, but now it is time to go deeper. Let me give you a gift that will awaken the vision of Śiva in your heart." Ānāya fell to the ground in full prostration. Tears welled up in his eyes not of sorrow, but of overwhelming joy. He touched the feet of the sage and said, "I have no other wish in my heart. I only long to reach the lotus feet of my beloved God Śiva. Please guide me. Please help me walk this divine path." The sage smiled. He raised Āṉāya with his hand and made him sit beside him under the banyan tree. "I shall initiate you into the Pañcākṣarī Mantra, the five-syllable mantra which is the very soul of Śiva. The mantra is 'Namaḥ Śivāya.' These five sacred syllables are not just sounds, they are the essence of the five elements, the five faces of Śiva, the five directions of awareness. Recite this mantra with every breath. Let it become your heartbeat." The sage then performed the ritual of Dīkṣā. He closed his eyes and chanted powerful prayers that purified the surroundings. He invoked Śrī Śiva and with the touch of his hand on Āṉāya's head, infused the mantra into his soul. "From today, you are no longer just a cowherd," the Sage declared. "You are a carrier of divine sound, a Sādhaka on the sacred path. Go, and sing the name of Śiva not only with your tongue, but with your whole being."

The Sage said to Ānāya, "In the beginning, Śrī Śiva initiated the gods Brahmā and Viṣṇu into Pañcākṣarī Mantra Dīkṣā. It was during the time when Śiva appeared as the infinite pillar of fire between them. Both sought to understand the truth of Mahādeva. Moved by their sincere search, Śrī Śiva bestowed upon them the divine knowledge of the Pañcākṣarī Mantra. This mantra is none other than the very form of Śiva himself. By chanting this mantra, one attains divinity from within." He continued, "You must chant the five-syllabled mantra

'Namah Śivāya' with unwavering faith. This mantra will gradually reveal to you the all-pervading presence of Bhagavān Śiva. Let it become the pulse of your breath, the rhythm of your life. Then, you shall truly understand what it means to see the world as filled with Mahādeva." Ānāya listened with deep attention. The Sage's words sank into his heart. With folded hands and tear-filled eyes, he bowed low before the enlightened sage. The sage, ever compassionate, placed his hand upon Ānāya's head once more and blessed him before quietly walking away into the forest.

From that moment, Ānāya's life transformed completely. His soul became absorbed in the holy name of Śiva. His lips continuously moved with the mantra 'Namah Śivāya'. His days and nights merged into the sound of divine remembrance. In the early hours of morning, when the world was still asleep, Ānāya would sit in stillness and chant the mantra 32,000 times. Only after completing this sacred practice, he would go out to tend his cows. Cows were his simple companions. They walked alongside him to the forests. But something in Ānāya had changed. Though outwardly he performed the same duties like milking the cows, preparing curd and ghee, offering to the temple, but inwardly he was immersed in bliss. The mantra echoed within him with every breath. Even while walking, collecting milk, or speaking to others, the Japa continued within. Gradually, he began experiencing a state of bliss that words could not describe. A sense of peace and unity pervaded his being. The trees he passed by, the rivers he sat beside, the wind that brushed past his cheeks, all appeared to him as forms of Mahādeva. He realized the truth of the saying, "Sarvaḥ Śivamayaṃ jagat" the whole world is pervaded by Śiva.

The illusion of duality began to fade. The Maya (illusion) of Maheśvāra seemed to dissolve under the light of the mantra. His eyes now beheld everything as the cosmic play of Mahādeva. His cows appeared to him as the sacred bull Nandi. The soft breeze of the forest felt like the winds from Mount Kailāśa. Every leaf, stone, and stream became a manifestation of the Lord he loved. People of the village noticed a change in him. His words became filled with wisdom far beyond his age. He spoke rarely, but whenever he did, it carried the depth of realization. Those around him admired his devotion, though many could not fully grasp the extent of his transformation. Still, he remained the same simple cowherd in his actions. He continued to serve the temple, offering the best milk, curd, and ghee. He never missed a single ritual. He still considered himself a humble servant of Śrī Śiva. And yet, the power of his mantra japa created a positive aura around him that could be sensed even by those unaware of spiritual matters. Animals too were drawn toward him. Birds would perch near him and sing. Deer would gather around him without fear. Even wild animals like lions and tigers that roamed the jungle never harmed him or his cows. There was a divine energy protecting him, an invisible shield created by the Mantra's power.

One day, Ānāya sat by the banks of a river, lost in the mantra's repetition. On either side of the river, the forest stood tall and silent. Time slipped by unnoticed. The sound of water and the hum of the mantra became one. He slipped into a deep state of meditation. The barriers between the individual and the divine dissolved. In that moment, he realized the highest truth, he was not different from Śiva. He saw himself in Śiva, and Śiva within him. The mantra had carried him beyond all illusions, into the heart of the cosmos. He saw the dance of creation, preservation, and dissolution as the play of his beloved Lord. As he remained in this state, one of his cows approached and began licking his feet. Slowly, awareness of the physical world returned. He looked at the cow with love and smiled. He remembered that he had to return to the village. But something in him had shifted forever. He now understood that Parakailāśa the supreme abode of Śiva, is not just a place in the cosmos. It exists everywhere, the Lord pervades all. Only a devotee can realise. Śiva exists in every breath, every sound, and every corner of existence. He reflected, "One who knows this becomes free from saṃsāra. He is united with Paramāśiva." Through the power of mantra, by the grace of the guru, and due to his unwavering faith, Ānāya attained the highest state of realization. People now looked up to him with deep reverence. Other devotees of Śrī Śiva came to him for guidance. They knew that he was no ordinary cowherd. The Lord himself stood behind him.

Despite all admiration, Ānāya remained humble. He never let pride enter his heart.

He continued to walk barefoot, serve the temple, tend his cows, and chant the mantra. In the sacred heights of Kailāsa, Śrī Śiva watched everything. The Supreme Lord knew the greatness of his devotee. With eyes full of love, he desired to bless Ānāya in a way that the entire world would know his glory.

Chapter 3

Divine Gift by Śiva

With each passing day, Ānaya Nayanār's love for Śrī Śiva deepened like the endless ocean. There was no day in his life when he did not offer selfless service to the devotees of Śiva. His hands were constantly engaged in charity, his voice in chanting, and his mind in remembrance of the Supreme. He followed a simple path, which was to serve the devotees, offer the best of what he had to the Lord, and keep chanting the sacred Pañcākṣarī Mantra "Namaḥ Śivāya." But this sacred mantra was not the only one that danced on his lips. Ānaya would often recite various holy names of Mahādeva with great love and reverence. These were not mere words to him, they were life itself. As he herded his cows through forests and fields, the air would be filled with his soft chants.

"शिवं शंकरं गौरीशं नीलकण्ठ त्रिलोचन महेश्वरं महादेवं त्रिपुरान्तक धूर्जटे कालाशासन कामारे कालकण्ठकलाधर, करुणालय पाहीति सदा भक्त्या प्रजल्पति"

"Śiva Śaṅkara Gaurīśa Nīlakaṇṭha Trilocana Maheśvara Mahādeva Tripurāntaka Dhūrjaṭi Kālaśāsana Kāmārī Kālakānta Kāladhara Karuṇālaya.....With devotion, he always used to say, 'Protect me."

Every name flowed from his heart like a sacred river, washing away the dust of worldly thoughts. He knew the power of each of these names. To Ānaya, chanting was not a ritual, it was process of union with the Supreme Lord. It was his lifeline. It was his bridge to the eternal. He often prayed in solitude, "O Śiva, O Compassionate one, please protect me! Let me never forget your name. Let my breath carry you within, in life and beyond." In his inner world, Paramaśiva was not some distant deity residing in an unreachable realm. He was near, closer than the breath, closer than thought. He was everything, the cows, the forest breeze, the milk he offered, the sacred mantra, everything was Śiva. But on the other side, seated upon the snowy peaks of Mount Kailāśa, Śrī Śiva the eternal Yogī, the Universal Being, the one with infinite eyes, infinite faces, infinite forms, was silently observing. His vision beyond time and space fell upon the earth and reached the heart of his devotee. Mahādeva is the supreme witness. He sees all. Not just the deeds, but the intentions behind them. He does not look merely at rituals; He looks at the bhava the feeling of surrender and devotion. In the humble heart of Ānaya, he saw a flame burning brighter than a thousand Yajñas. That flame was pure love. Śiva was moved. In the deep silence of his divine abode, he thought, "My devotee Ānaya has given me everything, his time, his strength, his service, his love. I must bless him in a way that will honour his devotion." Mahādeva is not just a destroyer of ignorance, he is a giver of grace. He is Āśutosha the one who is easily pleased by true devotion. The Lord desired to offer Ānaya a divine gift that would elevate his soul further and allow him to express his love in a new and beautiful way. He thought, "Let his devotion take the form of music. Let him sing my name with the breath of melody." Śiva's gaze turned inward, and with the power of divine will, he summoned Devī Sarasvatī the goddess of wisdom, knowledge, and music.

Instantly, the air on Kailāśa shimmered with Ethereal effulgence. A white lotus bloomed in the sky, and upon it appeared Devī Sarasvatī, resplendent in white garments, glowing like the moonlight reflected on a calm river. She was seated gracefully, her four arms bearing the Veena, a Manuscript, a Rosary, and a Vessel of holy water. These are the symbols of purity and knowledge. Beside her stood a pure white Haṁsa (swan), a symbol of discernment. Mahādeva greeted her with a divine smile. Śiva spoke, "Devī Sarasvatī I have called you for a task that springs from my heart. On earth, there is a devotee named Ānaya. His devotion pleases me deeply. His love is boundless. I want to offer him a gift that will allow his devotion to sing." Sarasvatī listened to the God. Śiva continued, "I wish for you to bless him with a flute that will carry the melody of the Pañcākṣarī Mantra. Through this, he will express his love for me not just through words, but through music. Let him play my name in the wind." The Goddess smiled and said, "O Śaṅkara, your will is the eternal law. I shall do as you say. To bless such a pure-hearted bhakta is indeed a joy. Let the sound of the mantra flow through his breath. Let the flute become an instrument of devotion." With folded hands, she bowed to Śiva and prepared to descend to earth.

One quiet night, as the moonlight filtered softly through the thatched roof of his dwelling, Ānaya Nāyaṉār lay asleep after a long day spent tending to his cows and chanting the holy names of Śiva. The gentle night was peaceful, but what awaited him was a moment that would forever transform his path of devotion. In the depths of his sleep, a sudden light engulfed his inner vision. A dazzling, bright light appeared, so intense that even within the dream, Ānaya had to close his eyes momentarily. The light did not resemble the sun or fire. It was pure, divine, and filled with a spiritual brilliance that the world had never seen. From the center of this celestial glow, emerged a figure, majestic, graceful, and filled with a compassionate presence. It was Devī Sarasvatī the Goddess of Wisdom, Music, and Learning. She stood before him, draped in white garments, adorned with sparkling jewels that reflected divine light in all directions. Her serene face exuded compassion, and her eyes radiated a motherly love. She stood upon a blooming white lotus. A majestic Haṁsa the swan symbol of wisdom and discrimination stood close beside her. Each of her four hands held a divine object - the Veena, a rosary, a book, and a pot of nectar. Ānaya was stunned. He folded his hands and stood in reverence. His heart was overwhelmed, and his mind, for a moment, stopped functioning in awe of her divine beauty. Sarasvatī Devī smiled with motherly affection and said, "O noble soul, Śrī Śiva is pleased with your unwavering devotion, your service to his devotees, and your constant chanting of his names. He watches you with joy, and your name has spread to the divine realms. Śiva, who loves music and devotion, has expressed his wish for you to offer your love to him through music."

As she spoke, a luminous flute appeared in her hand. It was no ordinary instrument. It carried a soft brilliance and divine fragrance. Made from no earthly substance, it looked like it was crafted from pure celestial light. "This is not just a flute," she continued. "This is a blessing from Śiva himself. With this, you shall play the sacred Pañcākṣarī Mantra 'Namaḥ Śivāya.' Through this divine melody, your soul shall unite with Śiva's eternal presence. Your bhakti will echo across the heavens. Receive this as a token of Mahādeva's love for you." Then, with utmost grace, Devī Sarasvatī extended her hand and placed the divine flute into Ānaya's palms. As soon as he touched it, he felt a sudden surge of energy and joy. His soul was immersed in an inexplicable bliss, as though Śiva himself had entered his heart through the gift. Before he could speak or bow down again, the divine vision disappeared. The celestial light withdrew into the dream-space, leaving behind a serene silence. Ānaya suddenly woke up. His eyes opened wide. For a few moments, he sat still, trying to understand what had just happened. The quiet of the night still lingered. He looked around in the moonlight. Everything was as it was, his room, the soft rustle of leaves, and the distant call of cows. But something was different. Then his eyes fell upon something beside him, lying near his resting mat was the flute. The same divine flute that Sarasvatī Devī had given him in the dream. His hands trembled with awe as he picked it up. Its radiance and softness confirmed what he had seen. It was not a dream. It was real. The Goddess of Wisdom had truly visited him. Śiva had truly blessed him. His eyes welled up with tears. He brought the flute close to his chest and bowed in gratitude. This was no ordinary gift. It was a divine medium meant not for worldly music but to convey his devotion directly to the feet of Śrī Śiva.

From that moment, Ānaya cherished the flute with utmost love and reverence. He played it not as an artist, but as a bhakta offering his heart. The first time he placed the flute on his lips; he played the sacred syllables of Pañcākṣarī "Namaḥ Śivāya." Each note he played flowed with his love and tears. As the sound rose from the flute, his heart melted, his mind emptied, and only Śiva remained. Daily, when he went into the forests with his cows, he took the flute with him. While the cows grazed peacefully, Ānaya would sit under a tree and play the flute, softly chanting "Namaḥ Śivāya" in tune. The forest that once echoed with bird calls and wind now echoed with divine melody. The birds sat silently on the branches, enchanted by the sound. Animals drawn by the sweetness, approached with calm hearts. Trees, leaves, and flowers seemed to sway in rhythm. Even the wind flowed gently around him, carrying the music as an offering to the unseen Mahādeva in Kailāśa. The sacred sound of Pañcākṣarī on the flute carried purity, innocence, and surrender. It was as if nature itself participated in Ānaya's devotion. He no longer needed words. The flute became his voice, and its melody became his prayer. He played the flute not for fame, not for pleasure, but as an expression of his soul's longing for Śiva. His fingers moved with care, his breath carried bhakti, and his inner voice continuously whispered, "O Śiva, my Lord, my refuge, please accept this humble offering." Every time he played, tears of joy rolled down his cheeks. He was not in the forest; he was in Śiva's presence. Time faded away. The world disappeared. There was only music... and Mahādeva. He had no desire left. The divine flute had become the link between his inner being and the supreme Lord. And so, the story of Ānaya Nāyanār entered a new phase, where devotion took the form of music, and music became his path to the eternal feet of Śrī Mahādeva.

Āṉaya Nāyaṉār playing the
tune of Pañcākṣarī Mantra

Chapter 4

Magic of Flute

With a heart untouched by ego and a life rooted in simplicity, Āṉāya Nāyaṉār continued to live as an ideal servant of Śiva. Every breath of his being resonated with the Pañcākṣarī mantra "Namaḥ Śivāya." Music had become his deepest language of love, and his flute the sacred vessel through which his soul communed with the Divine. The flute that had once come to him through the grace of Devī Sarasvatī was now an inseparable part of his spiritual path. Unlike others who might have rejoiced in mere possession of such a celestial gift, Āṉāya never treated it as an object of pride. It was, to him, an extension of his devotion, a medium to serve the Lord through sound.

The melody he offered was not for entertainment. It was tapas, a silent fire of devotion offered through breath and intention. Every day, before the first rays of the sun lit up the horizon, Ānāya would rise from his humble mat. His first thoughts were always of Maheśvara, and his body, mind, and actions were aligned in the worship of his beloved Lord. His humility and sweetness were like cooling shade in the scorching forest of saṁsāra. But it was in the forest, under the wide-open sky and amidst the peaceful company of his cows, that Ānāya found his true spiritual sanctuary. Just as Gopāla Kṛṣṇa once stood amidst his cows and played the flute, so too did Ānāya. In his own sacred way, he became the Gopāla whose flute echoed with the syllables of the divine mantra. The forests, the trees, the streams, and the animals all bore silent witness to this divine communion. When he played, it was not just sound that emerged from his flute, it was devotion, it was surrender, it was his soul breathing the name of Śiva. The melody that flowed from his fingers and lips was soaked in Ananya-bhakti unwavering devotion. With every note, he lost his sense of body and mind and entered deep samādhi. The boundaries between him and the Supreme faded away. Time ceased to move. Only Namaḥ Śivāya remained. As days passed, this flute sādhana became his primary form of penance. With no yajña, no grand rituals, no scriptures, just the power of pure devotion and the music of Śiva's name, Āṉāya's inner light began to shine brighter. His energies became refined and elevated, and though his outer life remained simple, inwardly he had become like a blazing fire of tapas.

Then came that auspicious day, foretold only in the heart of Mahādeva. On this sacred morning, Āṉāya felt a strange yet serene urgency within him. As always, he woke up before dawn. He lovingly milked his cows and bathed in cool, clean water from the stream. After drying himself and donning fresh cloth, he sat in meditation and chanted the Pañcākṣarī mantra thirty-two thousand times without break. Every repetition was a garland of surrender placed at the feet of Śiva. Once his japa was complete, he walked slowly to the village temple with a pot of fresh milk in his hand. Entering the sanctum, he stood before the Śivaliṅga and poured the milk as an offering, whispering the mantra with folded hands. He did not know it would be the last time he stood in that temple. But there was no sadness, only peace, only love. He turned to the devotees present and offered his respects, bowing to each one as if bowing to Śiva in every heart. No one around him sensed what was to come, but in the realm beyond time, Śiva had already prepared the next act in this divine lila. With a calm heart and silent joy, Āṉāya left the temple, calling his cows, and began his final journey into the forest, unaware that the Lord of the cosmos was soon to arrive to receive the final notes of his sacred music. With his cows trailing gently behind, Āṉāya stepped into the quiet sanctuary of the forest. The soft breeze moved through the tall grass, and the early morning light streamed through the trees, bathing everything in a golden hue. But to Āṉāya, it was not just a forest, it was Śiva's sacred space, a temple without walls. Every leaf, every breeze, every chirping bird was to him a manifestation of his Lord. The beauty of nature was not separate from Śiva, it was Śiva. He brought his cows under the shade of a massive banyan tree. Anāya then walked a few steps ahead and found a sturdy tree for support. He closed his eyes for a moment and invoked the image of Śiva in his heart. Standing in the graceful Tribhaṅgī Mudrā, Anāya looked like Kṛṣṇa. He had placed a peacock feather in his hair, an act not of imitation, not as decoration, but as a mark of simplicity and harmony with nature. His heart was singularly fixed on Mahādeva.

Inwardly, he imagined Śiva standing before him, listening. "My Lord," he thought, "may this humble melody reach your ears. May it please You. May it dissolve my ego and merge me into You." With that prayerful thought, he lifted the flute to his lips. His fingers rested lightly on its holes.

Then, he began to play. The sound that emerged was not of this world. It was the melody of the Pañcākṣarī Mantra, carried not by mere wind but by devotion that had ripened through years of surrender. With each gentle blow into the flute, Āṉāya breathed "Na... Ma... Śi... Vā... Ya...." The mantra was no longer just a chant on his tongue; it was the very breath of his life, flowing through the flute and out into the universe. As the tune flowed into the forest, everything began to respond. The cows lifted their heads and turned toward the sound, standing still in rapt attention. Trees that had long been barren suddenly sprouted green leaves. Flowers bloomed in every direction, painting the forest floor in vibrant colours. Fruits ripened instantly, dangling from branches as offerings to the unseen Lord. Wild creatures ordinarily filled with fear or aggression were drawn by the music. A tiger sat beside a deer; a snake curled up near a mongoose. Lions, peacocks, rabbits, boars, all gathered in silence. The laws of nature had momentarily paused. The tune of devotion had erased all enmity. Every creature, big or small, became a seeker of that divine sound. The rivers swelled with joy. Their waters, flowing rapidly a moment ago, began to slow. The streams appeared to stop mid-flow, as though the rivers themselves were holding their breath to hear one more note. Even stones began to melt, their hard forms softening under the effect of the sacred music. As Āṉāya continued to play, his consciousness dissolved even further. He was no longer aware of his body. His identity faded. Only Śiva remained, the eternal listener, the cosmic dancer, the Supreme recipient of his love.

The Devatās in the heavens felt the tremors of this devotion. From Brahmā to Indra, from Sarasvatī to Gaṇeśa, all turned their gaze to Earth. The Devas descended invisibly, surrounding the forest in a luminous glow, eager to witness the bhakta whose music was powerful enough to stir even the silence of space. Each note from Ānāya's flute was soaked in Ānanda, in spiritual bliss. The sky itself became heavy with presence, as if it too were leaning down to listen. Far above, in Kailāsa, Śrī Śiva sat in deep stillness beside Devī Śakti. But this stillness was stirred, not by war, not by yajña, not by philosophy, but by the sincere longing of a bhakta. The tune touched the ears of the Supreme. Śiva opened eyes and his face was filled with wonder. His gaze softened. His heart, though always full of compassion, now overflowed with affection.

The music of the flute woven with the mantra of his own name had pleased. Beside him, Śakti smiled and said, "O Lord of all beings, listen… the tune of Pañcākṣarī is calling You with pure devotion. That one is not merely playing; he is offering his soul with every breath. You must bless him." Śiva nodded with joy and said, "Yes, Devī. The time has come. Let us go. He shall receive the fruit of his unwavering love." Then, in a moment, Mahādeva rose, sat on bull Nandi, and began his descent to Earth. Devī Śakti joined him. The forest below was about to witness a divine visitation a meeting of devotee and Lord, soul and Source, yearning and fulfilment. The sound of the divine flute continued to drift across the forest, flowing through trees and rivers like a sacred offering. The sky, though vast and silent, seemed to hum with the same mantra. All beings had stilled, their hearts resting in the sacred resonance of "Namaḥ Śivāya." It was into this sacred stillness that Śrī Śiva descended, seated on Nandi, accompanied by Devī Śakti. As they reached the forest where Āṇāya stood lost in bliss, the very earth beneath them was sanctified. The grass swayed not with the wind, but in joy. The trees that had already blossomed now seemed to bow, their branches became aromatic with fragrance. The celestial beings, having never seen such a moment before, stood motionless in awe. Śiva's three eyes glowed with compassion, joy, and divine pride. His matted locks shimmered like waves of twilight, the crescent moon shining brighter in his hair. Devī Śakti seated beside him, appeared like a river of grace flowing from the source of all compassion. Together, they looked upon Āṇāya who was unaware of their presence. He remained absorbed in the ecstasy of his offering. Aṉāya stood motionless, the flute gently pressed to his lips, his body in perfect stillness, like a temple pillar, yet alive with energy. His inner sight beheld only Śiva. In his mind, he had long ago surrendered. In his heart, he had already merged. What remained now was only the final recognition by the Lord himself. Śiva did not speak immediately. He simply listened, as a devotee listens, as a friend listens, as the Supreme listens to the voice of love that asks for nothing. Every note of the flute was a syllable of surrender. Every breath was an offering. Every pause was filled with longing. Every sound was wrapped in silence. Finally, when the melody reached its last note, when the final breath of "Namaḥ Śivāya" gently passed through the bamboo and dissolved into the wind, Śiva stepped down from Nandi. He approached slowly, with quiet steps, as though not to disturb the sanctity of what had just occurred. Standing before the still-tranced bhakta, Śiva's heart swelled with love. The time had come. The final blessing was near. Raising his hand, Śiva looked at Aṇāya and said with a voice that echoed through all three worlds, "Come to My eternal abode." In that very moment, the power of mokṣa descended like a wave of golden light. Flowers began to shower from the heavens. The Devatās in the sky offered their praises, and the Ṛṣis folded their hands in reverence. The body of Aṇāya remained standing in Tribhaṅgī Mudrā, flute in hand, eyes half-closed, a gentle smile on his lips. He attained liberation, his soul became free from all bonds and soared high led by Śiva's grace towards the eternal realm of

Parakailāśa. There, in the divine abode where no sorrow can ever enter, Āṉāya took his place among the greatest devotees of Śiva. He had not attained mokṣa through scholarly learning, nor by austerities, nor by powerful rituals. He had attained it through devotion, through seva, through music, and through unwavering love. Nandi announced, "A true bhakta has been received by the Lord." Śiva turned one last time toward the earthly form of Āṉāya, now bathed in divine glow, and smiled. Devī Śakti too gazed compassionately upon the one whose bhakti had moved even the immovable. Āṉāya got merged into Śiva. Having completed his divine purpose, Śiva mounted Nandi once again. Accompanied by Śakti, the Lord returned the Golden Hall of Chidambaram, where he dances in bliss as Naṭarāja the cosmic dancer. But even in his dance, one could sense a new sweetness, as though the notes of Āṉāya's flute had merged forever into the rhythm of the cosmos. From that day onward, Āṉāya Nāyaṉār was remembered not just as a devotee, but as the one who made the flute itself a medium of mokṣa. His story echoed through the hearts of other seekers, inspiring them to realize that bhakti born of humility, love, and selfless service alone can attract the gaze of Mahādeva. And thus ends the earthly chapter of Āṉāya's journey, in the eternal resonance of "Namaḥ Śivāya", carried forever on the winds of devotion.

Bhagavān Śiva and Parāśakti looking at
Āṉaya Nāyaṉār compassionately

Chapter 5

Śiva Pañcākṣarī

Oṃkāra is not merely a sound. It is the primal vibration, the cosmic resonance that was born from the mouth of Śrī Śiva himself. It is said that the first sound ever heard in creation was the syllable "Oṃ," and from this sacred sound, the entire universe began to unfold. Among all mantras, Oṃ is supreme. It is the essence of Śiva, the sound form of the formless. Śiva is known as Oṃkāreśvara the Lord of Oṃ. There is no distinction between Oṃ and Śaṅkara. Just as a name signifies the one it belongs to, Oṃ is the sound that points directly to Śiva. In fact, it is said in the scriptures that Śiva himself is the sound Oṃ, and when a devotee utters it with awareness, he is calling upon the Lord in his purest, subtlest form. Vedas declare that the Supreme Brahman, the ultimate truth expounded by them, is none other than Śiva himself. Therefore, when Oṃ arises from the mouth of Śrī Śiva, it is the self-expression of the Absolute Reality. It is for this reason that the sacred Jyotirliṅga in Madhya Pradesh is known as Oṃkāreśvara. This Śivaliṅga is a living testimony to the unity of sound and form, nāda and rūpa, mantra and Devatā. Pilgrims come to this sacred spot to experience the divine fusion of Śiva and the primal sound. Oṃkāra is not separate from Śiva. In fact, it is Śiva in motion, Śiva as vibration, Śiva as that which awakens the sleeping soul. The sound of Oṃ has the power to elevate the soul. It is said that chanting Oṃ with devotion and understanding can bring a person closer to mokṣa, the final liberation. It bypasses the complexity of rituals, and touches the soul directly. It is pure, potent, and transcendent. In the Śiva Purāṇa, the Lord himself declares, "I am indicated by the mantra Oṃ." This statement alone reveals the secret. Oṃ is not just a symbol; it is the soul of Śiva. If a person, even unknowingly, chants "Oṃ," he is calling out Śiva. Even if he does not know that Oṃ represents Śiva, his lips are uttering the most sacred name of the Lord. This is the boundless compassion of Śrī Mahādeva, he accepts even the unknowing seeker.

But Oṃ is not just one sound. It is composed of five sacred elements: A-kāra, U-kāra, Ma-kāra, Bindu, and Nāda. These five parts hold within them the entire range of cosmic vibration. Each part is associated with one element of the universe, and together they form the full body of praṇava.

But even more mysteriously, these five components are reflected in the Pañcākṣarī Mantra Namaḥ Śivāya which is the most beloved of all mantras dedicated to Śiva. The five syllables of this mantra are: Na Ma Śi Va Ya. Each of these syllables is not random, each is rooted in the cosmic blueprint of sound. Na is derived from A-kāra, Ma is from U-kāra, Śi is from Ma-kāra, Va is from bindu, and Ya is from nāda. Thus, Pañcākṣarī Mantra is Oṃ in its expanded, gross form. In the words of the Śiva Purāṇa, Oṃ is the sūkṣma praṇava (the subtle sound), while Namaḥ Śivāya is the sthūla praṇava (the gross sound). One is the seed, the other the blooming flower. But both are inseparably connected. This is why chanting "Namaḥ Śivāya" is not just a repetition of five syllables, it is an entry into the secret of the cosmos. It is Oṃ revealed, Oṃ blossomed.

And just as Oṃ lifts the soul upward, so does the Pañcākṣarī Mantra. It connects the jīva (individual soul) to Śiva, the Paramātmā.

The essence of all scriptures, all mantras, all yajñas is found in this one mantra. The sages declare, "By the very remembrance of this, one attains liberation." Every mantra in the Vedas, every sacred formula used in rituals, has its origin in this mantra. Even the famous Gāyatrī Mantra known for its power is said to have emerged from the Pañcākṣarī. It is the womb of mantras, the heart of the śāstras. One who chants Namaḥ Śivāya with faith gains the merit of chanting crores of other mantras. Śrī Śiva is pleased easily, and this mantra is the most direct way to please him. Not only does Śiva grant worldly comforts like peace, health, protection, but he also grants the ultimate boon of liberation. Yet, as powerful as it is, the mantra is not to be treated lightly. The scriptures caution that Pañcākṣarī should be received through proper initiation (mantra dīkṣā). The mantra holds divine fire; without the guidance of a Guru, it can be misused or misunderstood. A guru in the Śaiva tradition is the living embodiment of Śiva, and receiving the mantra from such a guru is to receive it directly from the Lord himself. However, for those not yet initiated, all hope is not lost. They may chant the name of Śiva with love, and that too will bring immense blessings. Śiva's names are equally powerful. Names like Śiva Śiva, Śiva Śambhu, Sāmbasadaśiva, Mahādeva and Arunachal Śiva. These holy names vibrate with the same love. Even if one says, "Mahādeva" thrice with devotion, Śiva's attention is drawn. He recognizes his bhakta among millions just as the moon shines distinct among stars, or a firefly glows among others, the devotee who chants his name shines in Śiva's sight.

There is a story in the Purāṇas. Once, Brahmā and Viṣṇu got the knowledge of Pañcākṣarī Mantra from Śiva. They knew that this was not just a collection of syllables, but the key to divine realization. Śiva ever compassionate lord sat beside Devī Pārāśakti, facing the uttara (north) direction, he placed his hand gently upon their heads. With love and sacred intent, he whispered the Pañcākṣarī into their ears. From then on, they began to worship Śiva using that mantra. In their hymns and praises, they addressed him as:

Praṇavavācya - He who is described by Oṃ

Praṇavaliṅga - He who is in the form of Oṃ

Thus, even the highest gods, creator and preserver of the universe, knew that without the mantra, there is no path to Śiva. They submitted themselves, just as any seeker must do. Śiva is revered as Praṇava Oṃ the eternal sound, the first vibration of creation. It is for this reason that Brahmā and Viṣṇu address him as Praṇavavācya - the one who is described by the sacred syllable Oṃ, and Praṇavaliṅga - the one who is in the sound Oṃ. He is not only the source of Praṇava but also the very embodiment of it. The gross Praṇava is expressed in the five-syllabled mantra, known as the Pañcākṣarī Mantra - Na, Ma, Śi, Va, and Ya. This mantra represents the manifest form of Śiva. When the subtle form of praṇava, the sound Oṃ is prefixed to this mantra, it becomes the

Ṣaḍākṣarī Mantra or six-syllabled mantra: Oṃ Namaḥ Śivāya. This union of the subtle and the gross embodies both the transcendent and the immanent aspects of Mahādeva. The practice of this mantra, especially in its complete Ṣaḍākṣarī form, requires initiation (dīkṣā) from a qualified and realized guru. Without proper initiation, the inner potential of the mantra remains dormant. The guru's touch is the divine spark that ignites the fire of mantra within the heart of the disciple. In the sacred Śiva Purāṇa, a revered narrative unfolds in which Brahmā and Viṣṇu, after receiving divine knowledge from Śiva, praised him with profound stutis. They bowed and exclaimed:

"Salutations to You, O Śiva the formless One! Salutations to Niṣkalateja the radiant Lord without form! Though You are beyond form, you appear in divine form out of compassion. You are the eternal owner of the universe, Sakalanātha. You are Praṇavavācya and Praṇavaliṅga. We bow to you, the Lord whose essence is praṇava!" Their glorification continued: **"You are the first, Ādideva the primordial God, the original source of all creation. O Pañcamukha, five-faced Lord, you create, preserve, destroy, conceal, and liberate. You manifest as Pañcabrahma - Brahmā, Viṣṇu, Rudra, Maheśvara, and Sadāśiva. Through these divine aspects, you perform the pañcakṛtyas the five-fold cosmic acts. You are the ātman, the Self of all beings, the Brahman described in the Upaniṣads. You are truth, without decay, and possessor of countless divine qualities. O Śambhu! You are both sākāra (with form) and nirākāra (formless). You are the first teacher, the**

Ādiguru, the supreme preceptor, the silent teacher beneath the banyan tree. All other gods became your disciples. Even the great sages attained the knowledge of the Self by your grace alone. We bow again and again to you." Śiva, moved by their humility and sincerity, instructed Brahmā and Viṣṇu to worship his formed aspect with the Pañcākṣarī Mantra. He clearly stated that for the formless aspect, one must worship with praṇava (Oṃ), and for the manifest form (mūrti), and for the gross Praṇava, Pañcākṣarī should be used. This important teaching reveals a sacred balance. Oṃ being subtle, suits meditation on the formless Brahman, while Namaḥ Śivāya being more accessible and tangible, is perfect for worshipping Śiva's iconographic form. Śiva eventually disappeared after revealing the mysteries of both praṇava and Pañcākṣarī to

Brahmā and Viṣṇu. The knowledge was given by Śivā, but with the understanding that it was sacred and not to be used without reverence or initiation. The power of internal chanting, known as Mānasika japa. Among the types of japa (repetition of mantra), this form done silently within the mind is considered the most potent. If one chants without making any external sound but remains completely focused inwardly, it produces greater spiritual merit than even vocal repetition. When the chanting is audible to others, it is called Vācika japa, and when whispered or murmured so only the chanter can hear it, it is Upāṃśu japa. However, of all these, Mānasika japa is the most subtle and powerful, since it keeps the mind fully engaged in divinity. This mirrors the devotional practice of Ānaya Nāyaṉār. Whenever he played his divine flute, producing the melody of the Pañcākṣarī Mantra, he did not merely offer external music, he combined it with internal chanting. As his fingers moved across the flute and his breath flowed through the instrument, his mind was constantly immersed in silent repetition of the mantra "Namaḥ Śivāya." This union of external melody and internal mantra was his highest form of sādhana. This sacred coordination,flute as nāda and mantra as bhava, created a bridge between the senses and the soul. Ānaya Nāyaṉār was not merely playing notes, he was invoking Śiva with every breath, and chanting Mānasika japa with every beat of his heart. His practice turned the forest into a temple and his body into a shrine. Through this continuous offering, he elevated his consciousness and approached the state where Śiva himself becomes visible to the devotee. But how does one reach such a state? Śiva has made it clear in scriptures that no soul can bear his radiance unless it has undergone deep spiritual transformation. His form is not grasped by ordinary perception; it is seen only when the inner self is purified, the mind is free of worldly desires, and the veil of ego is removed. To gain this purity, severe penance (tapas) is essential. One must restrain the senses, renounce selfish attachments, and perform intense spiritual disciplines. The biggest obstacles lie within - kāma (lust), krodha (anger), lobha (greed), moha (attachment), mada (pride), and mātsarya (jealousy). These inner enemies must be conquered. It is only after the destruction of these enemies, when the mind turns inward and the heart fills with yearning for Śiva, his presence can be experienced. The Siddhas and Ṛṣis have always taught that the path to Śiva lies through a burning desire to know him, a desire so strong that it consumes all lesser desires. This is precisely the path followed by Ānaya Nāyaṉār. His devotion was not mechanical; it was alive with emotion and love. Every act he performed, whether feeding the cows, donating milk and ghee to temples, bowing to fellow devotees, or playing the flute in solitude, was an expression of his surrender. His daily rituals continued even after receiving the flute from Goddess Sarasvatī. He never stopped offering milk at temples. He never stopped serving devotees. He considered every act, no matter how small, as an opportunity to express his love for Śiva. This harmony between outer ritual and inner worship is ideal. While some focus solely on temple rites and neglect inner growth, others abandon rituals thinking only meditation matters. But Śiva's path is integral, he accepts both the ritual worship (karma yoga) and the devotional worship (bhakti yoga). The chanting of the Pañcākṣarī Mantra, either mentally, silently, or aloud leads one closer to Śiva. But when that chanting is mixed with music, service, humility, and an intense longing, it becomes even more powerful.

Chapter 6

Greatness of Holy Name

In this age of Kali, the sacred scriptures and the words of enlightened Ṛṣis echo one supreme truth that is Nāma Smaraṇa chanting the holy name of God, the path to liberation. The Vedas, Upaniṣads, and the teachings of saints affirm that in this degraded age of Kaliyuga, where dharma is weak and the mind is restless, there is no method more effective, more accessible, or more profound than the remembrance of Bhagavān through his divine name. Among all the holy names, the name of Śrī Śiva holds a unique power that penetrates the heart and reveals the inner presence of the Divine. When one chants the name "Śiva," "Maheśa," "Rudra," or "Nīlakaṇṭha," something extraordinary happens within. The practitioner, even without the support of elaborate rituals or temple offerings, begins to feel a deep connection to the all-pervading presence of the Supreme. That which was unseen, hidden behind the veil of ignorance, starts to become visible, not to the eyes, but to the soul. The name awakens the divinity within the heart.

According to the Vedas, Rudra resides within the hearts of all beings. He is not merely an external deity sitting in the celestial heights of Mount Kailāsa, but the eternal witness seated within every creature, every breath, and every thought. He is the inner consciousness the Antaryāmī, whose subtle presence sustains all life. Yet, how many truly experience his presence? How many feel the touch of Śiva in their lives? The answer lies in Nāma Japa, the constant repetition of the holy name. Śiva by nature is Gupta or hidden. He does not reveal himself to all. He watches silently, observing the sincerity, devotion, and the longing of the heart. When a soul, humbled and pure, chants his name with love and unwavering faith, Śiva begins to respond. Through the vibrations of the mantra, his presence begins to vibrate within the chanter. The name becomes a bridge between the Jīva and Maheśvara. The holy name is not a mere word. It is Śabda-Brahma, divine sound. It is the manifestation of consciousness in the form of vibration. In truth, the name and the named (Nāmī) are not different. When we chant the name "Śiva," we are not just uttering syllables; we are invoking the very essence of the Lord. The name of Śiva is imbued with the same energy, power, and divinity as the Lord himself.

In the profound silence of one's inner self, the mantra "Namaḥ Śivāya" resounds as the call of the soul to its source. The Pañcākṣarī mantra, consisting of five sacred syllables like Na, Ma, Śi, Vā, Ya is said to represent the five elements earth, water, fire, air, and space. It purifies the body, mind, and soul. It aligns the seeker with the elemental forces of the universe, and leads him to the feet of Śiva, the one who transcends all elements. In Kali Yuga, this mantra is a lifeboat. Scriptures may fade, minds may wander, but the holy name survives. It travels through the air, it penetrates the sky, it enters the heart, and it dissolves ignorance. Though Śiva is Nirākāra formless, he has many forms, each adorned with a name. These names are not arbitrarily assigned. They are descriptions of his qualities, actions, and divine play. Śiva as Paśupati the Lord of all beings, Śiva as Nīlakaṇṭha, the one with the blue throat who swallowed poison to save the world, Śiva as Vīrabhadra the fierce protector of dharma, each name is a doorway to a particular form and aspect of the Lord. Chanting these names invokes the form. When we utter "Vīrabhadra," the mighty form of the Lord with weapons and wrath arises in the mind. When we chant "Śaṅkara," the benevolent aspect of the Lord emerges. In this way, names give life to form, and through form, the seeker arrives at the formless. Without the name, the form remains distant, and without the form, the name seems abstract. But through constant practice, the two become one.

It is also said that the Tāṇḍava dance of Śiva's dance is reflected even in the atom. Modern science, through its study of atomic structure, unknowingly reveals the divine pattern. Just as the nucleus is encircled by electrons in dynamic motion, Śiva too dances in every unit of existence. His movement, his vibration, is not limited to cosmic dissolution but occurs at every micro and macro level. He is in the star and in the stone, he is in the air that moves and in the stillness of death, he is not bound to the temple nor confined to the image, he is Sarvatra everywhere. But to realize this, one must chant. The tongue must become soaked in his name. The mind must become filled with his presence. When doubts arise, one must ask: What happens through this chanting? Is there any change? The truth is not always visible in a day or a week. But slowly, as a stream erodes stone, the name clears away the layers of Māyā. The world that once appeared solid and real starts to look like a passing dream. The devotee begins to see the entire cosmos as the play of Maheśvara. Each sound, each form, each movement, becomes a part of Śiva's Līlā. He who chants the name with every breath starts to breathe divinity. For him, the line between sacred and profane dissolves. A rock becomes a Śivāliṅga, a river becomes Gaṅgā, the forest becomes Kailāsa, the body becomes a temple, every act becomes worship. This is the transformation caused by Nāma Smaraṇa. A soul who sincerely chants "Namaḥ Śivāya" or any holy name of the Lord with love, with humility, and with one-pointed attention begins to see not just the form but also the formless Śiva. The mantra opens both eyes, one that sees form and one that sees essence.

It leads from Sākāra to Nirākāra, and from Nirākāra back to Sākāra. It teaches the seeker that both aspects of God are true and eternal.

Śiva is also known as Ananta Nāma the One with infinite names. Each name is a droplet of his infinite ocean of being. Reciting them is not a mechanical ritual. It is the unification of the self with the Supreme. The Ṛṣis who composed the Śiva Sahasranāma the thousand names of Śiva, did so from the depths of realization. Each name was a flower offered at the feet of the Divine. It is said that one who chants with love will be granted Darśan, not always externally, but within. The form may rise in meditation: white as camphor, with matted locks, crescent moon on the head, Gaṅgā flowing from his hair, a serpent coiled around his neck, seated in deep stillness on the Himalayas. Or perhaps, he may appear in fire, in light, in space, in dream, or in silence. But even if the form does not appear, the fruits of chanting are immense. The heart becomes soft, ego dissolves, and the desires fall away. The soul becomes anchored in peace. One feels guided, protected, and blessed by a subtle but powerful presence. This is Śiva. Let us remember, in this Kali Yuga, no austerity surpasses the chanting of the holy name. No ritual is more effective. No offering is more pleasing to Śiva than the heart that calls out to him again and again. In times of sorrow, chant his name. In times of joy, chant his name. In times of confusion, chant his name. Let the name become your companion, your teacher, your refuge.

In the end, when all else fails, the name will remain and the name will carry you to the feet of the one who is formless, multi-formed, nameless, and all-named Bhagavān Śiva the auspicious, the compassionate, the eternal. Nāma Smaraṇa the chanting of the divine name, is not merely a means of spiritual refinement; it is the very foundation of realization. Without chanting the name of God, there is no realization of the Nirankar (formless) Brahman, nor any enlightenment of the Sākāra (formed) aspect of the Divine. It is the Nāma that leads the aspirant from the seen to the unseen, from the tangible to the intangible, from the divine image to the eternal silence beyond form. Bhagavān Śiva himself, the ultimate source of all knowledge, has declared that the formless aspect of the Supreme must be worshipped through the vibration of Omkāra, also known as Pranava. This sacred sound composed of the syllables A-U-M is the seed of all creation and the breath of the formless Divine. In the sacred texts and Śāstras, it is repeatedly mentioned that Omkāra is none other than Śiva. The realization of Nirguṇa Brahman that which is beyond attributes, beyond form, beyond thought comes through the contemplation and chanting of Omkāra. It is subtle, transcendent, and leads the aspirant to merge with the infinite Śiva who pervades the void and fullness of the cosmos alike. Yet, for those whose minds still seek the divine Rūpa the sacred forms of the Lord, the chanting of the Pañcākṣarī mantra, "Namaḥ Śivāya," is the way. It is the Sthūla Praṇava the gross or manifested form of Omkāra as described in the Śiva Mahāpurāṇa. This mantra is not lesser than Om; it is the bridge through which the gross mind ascends to the subtle, the manifest to the unmanifest.

Ānāya Nāyanār the great devotee,constantly recited the Pañcākṣarī mantra. His longing was for the Sākāra Darśana of Mahādeva. He did not seek formless abstraction; his love demanded the presence, the smile, the glance, the grace of the Lord in divine form. And indeed, Śiva responded. Appearing in glorious effulgence, seated upon Nandi with the Divine Mother Śakti beside him, Śiva granted mukti (liberation) to his devoted servant. This event is not merely a tale of the past but an eternal truth. It signifies that chanting the holy name leads directly to the presence of the Lord, whether one seeks the Rūpa or the Arūpa, the form or the formless. But one must ask: Why is chanting so effective? Among all paths like rituals, meditation, austerities why the chanting of the divine name holds such exalted status?

The answer lies in its ability to transform the human mind. The mind, being restless and scattered, finds stillness only when anchored to a divine vibration. Chanting becomes the anchor. With each repetition of the name "Śiva," the waves of thought begin to settle. The noise of the world begins to fade. The presence of Śiva begins to arise. The mind, thus purified, becomes capable of perceiving what was once hidden. Śiva reveals himself in a pure mind and in illumined intellect. This illumination is not achieved by mere intellectual study or external rituals alone. Unless the power of the holy name is awakened from within, no amount of outer worship bears fruit. The name, when chanted consistently, begins a sacred journey within the body of the Sādhaka. Initially, the name enters only as sound, through the mouth. If the seeker continues his Japa with sincerity and devotion, the mantra begins to vibrate not only in the throat but starts descending inward, towards the heart. This sacred descent is not metaphorical. It is real. It is experiential. As the holy name moves from the lips to the throat, and from the throat to the heart, the Antaryāmī Śiva begins to shine within. That shining is not light alone, it is Ānanda, pure bliss. All sins are burned in the fire of Nāma. But more than sin-removal, the name bestows the highest treasure Antarānanda the inner bliss of union with the Supreme. The Vedas say that where there is a pure heart, there Śiva dwells. The chanting of the name connects with the very pulse of the devotee. It moves with the breath. It resonates with every heartbeat. And when this resonance reaches a peak, a nectar begins to flow. The seeker tastes the rasa of divine presence. It is a sweetness that no worldly pleasure can match.

The journey of the holy name is threefold: vāchika (verbal), upāṁśu (whispered), and mānasika (mental). In the beginning, one chants aloud. Slowly, the chanting becomes more internal, more intimate, more subtle. Even in silence, the name reverberates within. One should never abandon the holy name, even when the form of God appears before one's eyes. Ānāya Nāyaṉār continued playing his flute in front of Śiva himself. In ecstasy, he did not stop his Nāma Smaraṇa. He kept chanting internally, even as his beloved lord stood before him. This teaches us a profound lesson. Divine Darśana is transient if not sustained by inner remembrance. Nāma is the thread that binds the soul to the Supreme. The same was practiced by Jagadambā Pārvatī herself. Before she became the consort of Śiva, she undertook intense penance. It was Sage Nārada who initiated her into the Pañcākṣarī mantra. She accepted it not as a ritual but as her very life-breath. Through snow, sun, wind, and hunger, she continued her chanting with unwavering focus. Seeing her resolve, Śiva wished to test her. He sent the Saptarṣis the seven great sages, to distract her. They came with logic, stories, and warnings. "Why do you waste your youth in tapas?" they asked. "Śiva is a detached ascetic. He will not marry. Nārada has misguided you." But Pārvatī remained unshaken. With calm firmness, she replied that her devotion was not based on promises or outcomes. It was rooted in Śraddhā deep faith and Nāma Smaraṇa. She said, "Even if Śiva does not accept me, I shall continue chanting his name. That is enough for me." Then came another test. Śiva himself appeared, disguised as a wandering ascetic. He spoke harshly about himself, "Why do you seek Śiva? He lives in cremation grounds. He smears ash on his body. He is strange and frightening. Why waste your life on such a being?" But Pārvatī the embodiment of Śakti and devotion, refused to listen to any Śiva Nindā criticism of the Lord. She declared that none but Śiva could be her Lord. The mantra "Namaḥ Śivāya" had become her identity. When the seven Ṛṣis and Śiva disguised as a wandering ascetic, attempted to shake the resolve of Devī Pārvatī, they failed. Rather, their tests only intensified her inner fire. When the Sage mocked Mahādeva and uttered harsh words against him, Pārvatī could no longer bear the blasphemy. Filled with divine rage and unwavering Śraddhā (faith), she rose and departed from that place. Her fury was not born of ego but of deep devotion that refused to accept any insult against her Lord. This was the final test. Śiva, pleased with her love and unwavering chanting, revealed his true form, and accepted her as his consort. He was resplendent, calm, radiant like millions of suns, yet soothing as the cool rays of the moon. The Lord of all creation stood before her not as a distant deity but as her eternal companion. In that sacred moment, the tapas of Pārvatī bore fruit. Her unwavering mantra-japa, her adherence to her Guru's instructions, and her single-pointed love resulted in their divine union. She attained Śiva as her husband. This episode, told in many Purāṇas, is not only the story of a goddess but a profound example of the path of Nāma Bhakti. Despite divine discouragement and intense testing, Pārvatī never abandoned her Mantra Japa. She followed the words of her Guru Nārada Muni, who was not only her initiator but also the beacon of her spiritual path. The grace of a true Guru when combined with the devotee's perseverance makes Śiva happy. Obedience to the Guru's word is the supreme spiritual discipline. Ānāya Nāyanār, too, embodied this ideal. He did not invent his path but walked upon the sacred trail shown by his Guru. His every breath carried the vibration of "Namaḥ Śivāya" and his heart was filled with the fragrance of the Lord's name. He is a shining example of what it means to be established in both action (karma) and contemplation (dhyāna) through the power of the holy name.

The lesson here is eternal. Nāma bhakti transcends even the trials of the gods. It survives doubt, opposition, hardship, and tests. It leads to union, to joy, to completeness. Let us understand one final truth. Śiva in his nirākāra form is often represented as the Śivaliṅga. It is not a stone, but a symbol of the infinite formless Brahman. The worship of Omkāra leads one to merge in this undivided Sat-cit-ānanda. And the worship of the Pañcākṣarī leads one to the divine Rūpa of Śiva he who is beautiful, compassionate, fierce, and all-loving. But Realization of formless or formed is not possible without Nāma Smaraṇa. The name is the Bīja (seed), the Mārga (path), and the Phala (fruit). Thus, whether one seeks to dissolve into silence or to dance in devotion, the name is companion. All paths merge in the One who is both Nirguṇa and Saguṇa, both Śūnya and Pūrṇa, both silence and sound is Śrī Śiva. The world is not an easy place for steady remembrance. The Māyā of Mahādeva is powerful beyond measure. It is he who weaves the cosmic illusion, and it is also he who provides the way out. The same Śiva who binds with illusion, also liberates through Nāma. But the challenge is that the veil of illusion is so vast, so immersive, that beings do not even realize they have forgotten God. For hours, days, months, or even years, one may remain lost in worldly pleasures and obligations, oblivious to the soul's true calling. The forgetfulness is so deep that even the loss of remembrance goes unnoticed. Only when the name returns, when it touches the tongue again, when it vibrates within once more, the soul remembers what it had been missing. Worldly pleasures are fleeting, but their grip is strong. They distract, enchant, and delude. But the name of God is like a golden thread in the dark forest. When held firmly, it leads the soul home. A true devotee chants the name of Śiva with every breath. If he misses even a moment, he feels the void, the restlessness of separation. But when chanting becomes constant, the devotee sees Śiva with his eyes, but that the form of Śiva begins to dwell within the eyes themselves. Every sight reflects Śiva. Every moment becomes a mirror of the divine.

It is important to understand that true love for God arises through the influence of the holy name. Selfless love is not a product of mind, thought, or emotion. It is a fragrance released when the fire of Nāma Japa burns within. This love has no conditions. It is not born of fear or expectation. It flows like the Gaṅgā, purifying and liberating all it touches. The abode of Śiva does not need to be sought outside. It manifests within the heart that chants his name. The Śabda becomes the vehicle, and within it, the presence of Śiva begins to shine. A light arises not from any external lamp but from within the very soul. That light is Śiva. That joy, that Ānanda, is his gift. While there are many methods to approach the Divine. Rituals, pilgrimages, austerities, scriptural study none of them are effective if not done with Nāma Japa. Without the holy name, worship becomes mechanical. With the name, even silence becomes sacred. Through chanting, one receives not just devotion (Bhakti), but also wisdom (Jñāna), concentration (Dhyāna), and union (Yoga). All paths meet in Nāma. It is the seed, the tree, and the fruit of all

Sādhana. For the devotee, yoga is not merely postures or breath control. Yoga is the unite self with the Supreme. And the strongest rope that binds the soul to Śiva is the name. True yoga is remembering God at all the times. It is resting the mind at his feet. It is letting the waves of thought dissolve in the ocean of "Namaḥ Śivāya." A real Yogī is not one who abandons the world but one who carries the remembrance of Śiva in every act. In Kali Yuga, such Yogīs are rare. The age is full of confusion, indulgence, and distraction. People forget this supreme truth. But he who knows it, who holds to it, is a true Jñānī and bhakta. The summary of all scriptures, all stories, all teachings, is the name of God. The name is the essence, the support. Without the name there is no wisdom, no meditation, no worship, no liberation. Let every breath carry the name of

Śiva. Let the heart repeat it in silence. Let the tongue be soaked in its sweetness. Let the eyes see only him. Let the world be seen not as a burden but as his playground. When this state arises, the mind does not desire anything else. The soul rejoices, not in attainment but in the journey itself. Even if Śiva does not appear in form, the joy of chanting his name is enough. And when he does appear, as he did to Ānāya, it is only to bless the devotee who never stopped calling out. Such is the path. Simple yet supreme. Humble yet majestic. Invisible yet powerful. It begins with a whisper, Namaḥ Śivāya. It ends in union with the Infinite. In this world where the mind is tossed by desires, attachments, anxieties, and sorrows, there is one medicine that heals instantly and completely the divine name of God. Among all practices and disciplines, none can calm the restless heart and turbulent mind as swiftly as the chanting of Śiva Nāma. The mind may wander during rituals. The body may tire in long austerities. The intellect may be lost in scriptures. But a single heartfelt chant of "Śiva" can transform the inner space of the devotee into a sanctum of divine presence. The name of Śiva is not merely a sound. It is a flame, a vibration, a river of bliss flowing from eternity. The one who chants it with love feels its warmth and brilliance in the heart. Restlessness fades away. The mind, which was like a stormy sea, becomes calm like the still waters of a sacred lake reflecting the moonlight of Śiva's compassion. To one who is established in Nāma bhakti, Śrī Śiva is never invisible. The veil that hides the Divine from ordinary sight is torn apart by the sword of Nāma Smaraṇa. Every tree, every stone, every star, every breeze begins to speak the name of Śiva. The world, instead of appearing mundane, becomes alive with divinity. The devotee filled with love and purified by mantra sees the Lord's form in every direction. It is said that just as the river flows naturally to its destination, the divine form of Śiva follows the course of his name. Where there is Nāma, there Śiva appears. The formed aspect of God is inseparable from his holy name. The vibration of the name calls forth the presence of the Lord in his Sākāra form. As the devotee chants, a divine aura radiates from within, and the state of eternal Ānanda arises. Such a state is not understood by intellect. It is beyond philosophy and logic. It is a sacred madness known only to the one who attains it. The devotee laughs, cries, dances, and sings, intoxicated with the nectar of Nāma. He loses awareness of the external world and becomes absorbed in the inner presence. In such moments, the play of the ego ends. All desires fall away. The mind becomes blank, like a spotless mirror reflecting nothing but the light of Śiva. This is not a theory, it is a lived truth. But it cannot be explained, it must be experienced. The one who reaches that peak of devotion knows the secret, but even he cannot describe it fully. He can only sing, cry, and weep in joy, for words are too small to contain such vastness. There is no treasure greater than the name of God. There is no knowledge higher than the name of God. There is no Puṇya (merit) more sacred than the remembrance of the holy name. In truth, everything is the name of God. The Nāma is not different from the Nāmī the named. The name "Śiva" is Śiva himself. The name "Maheśvara" carries the very power of the Supreme. The repetition of the name invokes that power and makes it descend into the life of the devotee.

Even Siddhis supernatural powers can be attained through the repetition of the Divine Name, but the true devotee does not seek powers. He seeks presence. He seeks to dwell in the nearness of his beloved Lord, to be united in thought, word, and breath. What is truly astonishing is that even Śiva the Lord of the cosmos, is bound by his own name. He who cannot be bound by space, time, or causation, is moved by the sincere chanting of "Śiva." The name holds such immense force that Śiva is drawn to it like a bee to nectar. When a devotee chants with love, the Lord is compelled by the thread of bhakti to manifest. It is said that the name of Śiva is greater than Śiva himself. He who invokes Śiva by the name, Śiva reveals himself, and makes his form accessible to that devotee. He who chants "Śiva" becomes a beacon of divine light, drawing the attention and grace of the Lord of Kailāsa. The story of Sundaramūrti Nāyaṉār one of the most revered devotees of Śiva, beautifully illustrates this truth. Sundaramūrti, immersed in love and devotion, undertook pilgrimages to various Śiva Kṣetras (sacred sites of Śiva). He was never alone. His companions were not only fellow devotees, but also the holy name of Śiva, which he chanted constantly. The Pañcākṣarī mantra "Namaḥ Śivāya" was ever on his lips and in his heart. During one of his sacred journeys, Śiva himself decided to test and bless him. Disguised as a Brāhmaṇa, the Lord erected a shed along Sundaramūrti's path and offered food and water to him and his companions. After serving them, the brāhmaṇa mysteriously disappeared. Realizing that no ordinary person could have shown such spontaneous love and service, Sundaramūrti understood that it was Śiva himself. Later, after having Darśana in the temple, Sundaramūrti felt the pangs of hunger again. Śiva once more in disguise approached him and said, "You appear hungry. Wait, I shall get you some food." The Lord then went door to door, begging alms from householders, and returned with a sufficient offering. He lovingly served Sundaramūrti and all his companions. As soon as they finished eating, the Brāhmaṇa vanished. Once again, the realization struck. The server of food was none other than the one who is the provider of the universe. Sundaramūrti was moved beyond words. His eyes filled with tears, and his heart overflowed with gratitude. He composed and sang a song in praise of Śiva's compassionship, his humility, and his unconditional love for devotees. What was the secret of such divine interaction? It was Nāma. Throughout his journey, Sundaramūrti Nāyanār chanted the Pañcākṣarī mantra without pause. The constant remembrance attracted the Lord, invoked his form, and brought about these divine encounters.

This story mirrors the deeper truth that those who live in remembrance are never alone. God himself becomes their companion, guide, and servant. Just as Śrī Kṛṣṇa took the control of Arjuna's chariot and guided him through the war of Dharma. Similarly, the Lord takes charge of the life of one who chants his name with full surrender. The chanting of the holy name does more than attracting God, it awakens the divine within. Every soul is a spark of Śiva. But this spark remains dormant, hidden beneath layers of worldly dust. The act of Nāma Japa blows upon this hidden ember and kindles the inner flame. Slowly, the divine begins to radiate from within. The mind that was once scattered becomes focused. The heart that was once restless becomes still. The ego that sought separation dissolves in the ocean of unity. The eyes begin to see with compassion. The voice begins to speak only truth. The body moves in service of the Divine. This transformation is not an ideal, it is the natural result of chanting God's name. Therefore, let no one underestimate the power of the holy name. Not through knowledge, austerity, charity, or rituals alone, but through the remembrance of the name one attains liberation. In the end, when all philosophies collapse into silence, and all scriptures rest upon the tongue, the name alone remains. It is the beginning and the end, the seed and the fruit, the path, and the destination. Namaḥ Śivāya or the holy name of Śiva is the heartbeat of the soul.

Chapter 7

Bhasma and Rudrākṣa

In the boundless realms of time and space, where creation and destruction rise and fall like waves upon the ocean, one Supreme Reality Śiva stands unshaken. He is known as the Mahādeva, the Supreme Being who is beyond birth and death, beyond form and formlessness. He is the one who dances in the cremation grounds, who meditates in absolute stillness on top of Mount Kailāsa, and who grants liberation to the most fallen souls through his unmatched compassion. Among the many symbols and offerings that are inseparably connected with Śrī Śiva, two stand out with immense spiritual depth and divine mystery, Bhasma the sacred ash, and

Rudrākṣa the tear-born seed of the Lord himself.

Śiva is not bound by the constraints of time or the limitations of space. He is Sanātana, eternal. Even after the dissolution of the universe, when the Tri-lokas the three worlds, heaven, earth, and the netherworld vanish into void, Śiva remains. He is the witness of all, the silent seer, the substratum of existence and non-existence. Unlike all other entities subject to Saṁsāra, the endless cycle of birth and death, Śiva transcends the dualities of life. And in this transcendence, he offers a key to liberation, the understanding that everything except him is temporary. This fundamental truth is symbolically communicated through Bhasma.

Bhasma is the sacred ash that is dear to Śrī Śiva. It is not just any ash, but ash that is prepared from sacred substances, often cow dung or sacrificial remains, made pure by specific Vedic rituals. In appearance, it is simple. But in significance, it is profound. Śiva smears this ash on his body. On his arms, chest, forehead, and neck. Why would the Supreme Lord, who possesses all worlds, adorn himself with ashes? The answer is sublime. To remind all beings that everything in this world, body, wealth, name, and fame is ephemeral. The body, no matter how beautiful or strong, will one day turn to ash. Kings and beggars, saints, and sinners all meet the same fate. Bhasma is the great equalizer and awakener. But Bhasma is not merely a symbol of destruction; it is a purifier, a redeemer. By wearing it, one is not embracing death, one is embracing truth.

One is asserting that he or she belongs not to this perishable world, but to the imperishable reality Śiva.

The story of Rudrākṣa is equally wondrous. According to ancient Purāṇic tradition, Mahādeva once entered a deep state of meditation. He closed his eyes and contemplated his own auspicious form. In this eternal trance, thousands of years passed as the Lord remained in stillness. When Śiva at last opened his eyes, tears began to fall, not out of sorrow, but out of divine grace. These tears sacred beyond measure fell upon the earth. And wherever they touched the soil, Rudrākṣa trees sprouted. The seeds of these trees came to be known as Rudrākṣas. Thus, each bead of Rudrākṣa is not a mere ornament, it is a form of Śiva's compassion a seed of grace offered to the world for the purpose of spiritual upliftment. The one who wears it is brought under the direct protection of Rudra himself.

The spiritual magnitude of Bhasma is clearly revealed in the Bhasma Jabāla Upaniṣad a sacred text that contains the direct teachings of Śrī Śiva. In this Upaniṣad, Śiva declares, "He who smears his body with Bhasma with devotion to me, I shall free him from all sins. Even the worst of actions are purified by the touch of this sacred ash." Śiva himself explains the procedure for preparing and applying Bhasma. It must be sanctified through mantras and applied with reverence. The forehead is marked with three horizontal lines, known as the Tripuṇḍra. These lines are not decorative; they represent deep philosophical truths. The first line represents Brahmā the creator, the second line represents Viṣṇu the preserver. The third line represents Rudra the destroyer. By adorning the Tripuṇḍra, one affirms his allegiance to all three divine functions and ultimately to the Supreme Reality Śiva. In Śaiva tradition, it is considered auspicious to receive Bhasma from a Guru a realized preceptor who has merged his individuality with Śiva-consciousness. Just as initiation into mantra should come from the Guru, the sacred ash when given by a spiritual teacher carries the śakti (power) of divine transmission. It brings the seeker closer to Sambha Śiva the ever-auspicious Lord who dwells in all.

Smearing oneself with Bhasma is not limited by caste, gender, or age. In fact, all four varṇas Brāhmaṇa, Kṣatriya, Vaiśya, and Śūdra have the right to wear the Tripuṇḍra.

Women, widows, ascetics, and even children may apply the sacred ash. Śiva makes no distinctions. The one who wears the marks of Śiva becomes the living embodiment of Śiva. According to the scriptures, each particle of Bhasma is equal to one Śivaliṅga. That means, when a devotee applies Bhasma, they are not just adorning themselves, they are enshrining Śiva upon their body, countless times. One particle of Bhasma is one Śivaliṅga. A person who applies Bhasma carries innumerable Śivaliṅgas on his being. Even the dust of this ash, if applied with devotion, can liberate a soul from the grip of karma. The glory of Bhasma and Rudrākṣa is deeply intertwined with the nature of Śiva himself. They are not mere objects of worship. They are extensions of Śiva's grace. In them resides the message of detachment, purification, and transcendence. They serve as constant reminders that the eternal Self is our identity and not the temporary body.

The divine gifts of Bhasma and Rudrākṣa, though outwardly simple, are powerful tools for inner transformation. They are not only marks of Śiva's devotees but instruments of purification and gateways to liberation. Through proper understanding and application, these sacred elements align the Sadhaka's life with the divine current of Śiva-tattva. Practice of applying Bhasma to the body is both an act of devotion and a reminder of the eternal truths. In the Bhasma Jabāla Upaniṣad, Śrī Śiva describes the method of preparing the sacred ash. Sacred Ash made from burning of dried cow dung is called Agneya Bhasma. The most essential application is upon the forehead, where three horizontal lines are drawn using the thumb, middle, and ring finger, while chanting the Pañcākṣarī mantra. This mark is called Tripuṇḍra. Each of the three lines holds deep esoteric meaning. Thus, the Tripuṇḍra is not merely symbolic, applying it is an act of spiritual warfare against the forces that bind the Jīva (individual soul) to Saṁsāra. The forehead being the seat of the Ājñā cakra becomes energized with Śiva's śakti through the application of Bhasma. This sacred mark is not limited to the forehead alone. Many devotees apply Bhasma on the chest, arms, neck, and torso. Each application is accompanied by mantra and inner recollection of Śiva's presence. The more a devotee smears Bhasma, the more he dissolves his identification with the body and awakens to his true Self.

In the world of spiritual practice, Śiva stands as the great equalizer. Unlike rituals that may be reserved for specific Varṇas or communities, the application of Bhasma and the wearing of Rudrākṣa are open to all. According to the Śāstras and the Upaniṣads, men and women, young and old, householders and renunciates, and even widows and children are permitted and encouraged to wear the Tripuṇḍra and Rudrākṣa. This inclusivity stems from the truth that Śiva sees only bhakti, not birth. He sees only Śraddhā (faith), not social status. The one who wears the marks of Śiva becomes form of Rudra. The Śiva Mahāpurāṇa states that such a person, even if previously sinful, becomes adorable to the Devatās, including Brahmā, Viṣṇu, and Indra. In fact, those who do not wear Bhasma are warned in the same texts that they will not attain Jñāna of Śiva, even after crores of births. Such is the purifying power of these sacred symbols.

While Bhasma sanctifies the outer and inner body through destruction of tamas and attachment, Rudrākṣa beads help to stabilize the inner spiritual current. The wearing of Rudrākṣa is not merely an act of devotion but a complete sādhana. The Rudrākṣa is said to carry within it the vibration of the Śiva mantra. It acts as a spiritual antenna, constantly attuning the mind to higher frequencies. Touching it, seeing it, or even keeping it nearby purifies the environment and consciousness. Śiva Purāṇa emphasizes that damaged Rudrākṣas must not be worn. The beads should be whole, clean, and energized with mantra. There are Rudrākṣas with varying Mukhīs (faces), each having its own spiritual effects, from one-faced to twenty-one-faced, with the five-faced being most common for general use.

Every Sādhaka should wear Rudrākṣa Mālā around the neck, and optionally on the arms and wrists. When one chants Śiva Nāma using a Rudrākṣa mālā, the power of that japa is amplified manyfold. Śiva himself is said to reside in the Rudrākṣa bead. Therefore, the devotee who wears it is under constant divine protection. The Tripuṇḍra on the forehead and the Rudrākṣa mala around the neck do not merely indicate that one is a devotee of Śiva, they transform the bearer into a spiritual vessel. Just as a temple becomes sacred by the presence of a Śivaliṅga, the human body becomes sacred by the presence of Bhasma and Rudrākṣa. A verse from the Śiva Purāṇa declares, "Merely seeing a person adorned with Rudrākṣa and Bhasma destroys sins accumulated over many lifetimes." This means that the devotee himself becomes a Tīrtha, a place of pilgrimage. His presence purifies others. His glance bestows blessings. His body, though made of flesh, becomes Rudrarūpa the very form of Rudra. The path of Śiva is not just for individual liberation; it is for universal upliftment. A true devotee becomes a light for others, silently guiding them toward truth.

The power of Rudrākṣa is not only spiritual but also protective. The texts declare that evil spirits, ghosts, demons, and negative energies cannot stand in the presence of Rudrākṣa. Just as darkness flees from sunlight, these forces flee from the one adorned with Śiva's tear-born seed. By wearing Rudrākṣa and smearing Bhasma, one creates a spiritual armour around oneself. Even if one has committed sins, these sacred elements begin to burn away past karmas, preparing the soul for higher awareness. What to speak of devotees of Śiva, even devotees of Viṣṇu, Gaṇeśa, Durgā, or Sūrya benefit from wearing Rudrākṣa. The texts proclaim that all Devatās are pleased with a person who wears Rudrākṣa because he is already dear to Mahādeva.

One of the most profound aspects of Bhasma and Rudrākṣa is that they are natural, simple, and accessible. Unlike gold ornaments, expensive rituals, or complex mantras, these two are freely available and powerful. Śiva as Digambara, the one who wears no clothes but space, lives in simplicity. His message is clear that true wealth is not material, it is spiritual. By adopting the symbols of Śiva like the ash and the bead, a seeker aligns himself with the supreme power that governs, sustains, and dissolves the universe. He or she no longer walks as a limited being, but as a soul touched by eternity.

Bhasma and Rudrākṣa are the outward signs of an inward transformation. They are Śiva's way of marking those who belong to him. Through their use, the body becomes a temple, the mind a sanctum, and life itself a Yajña. Now, we shall dive into true stories from Chidambara Charitra, where these sacred elements brought about miraculous liberation, not only for humans, but even for animals by the grace of the ever-compassionate Mahādeva. The scriptures declare that the glory of Bhasma and

Rudrākṣa is limitless, and only Mahādeva himself knows its full extent. Yet, through the words of Saints and Sages, especially through works like Chidambara Caritra, glimpses of this boundless grace are revealed to us. These stories are not just accounts from the past; they are living truths that demonstrate Śiva's compassion, inclusiveness, and the power of his sacred symbols to liberate even the most fallen souls. There was once a man who strayed from the path of righteousness. He became involved in an illicit relationship with another man's wife. When the woman's husband discovered the affair, he was enraged beyond control. In a fit of fury, he killed that man, and the body of the slain man was cast out of the village. It was left abandoned and without any final rites. This occurred just before Mahāśivarātri the most sacred night dedicated to Śrī Śiva. As destiny would have it, there was a temple of Śiva in that very village, and preparations for the festival were underway. A large heap of Bhasma was gathered in the temple as part of the rituals. Unknown to the villagers, a stray dog entered the temple and sat in that pile of sacred ash, getting smeared with Bhasma in the process.

Later, as the dog wandered out in search of food, it walked near the place where the dead body of the sinner had been discarded. The dog stepped onto the corpse, and in doing so, some of the sacred ash fell from its body onto the lifeless form. That accidental contact with Bhasma, though seemingly insignificant, was spiritually monumental. In that very moment, all the sins committed by the man in his lifetime were burned away.

The touch of Śiva's sacred ash purified his astral body, removed the dark karmas that bound his soul, and freed him from the fate of wandering as a preta (spirit). His body merged into the five elements, and his soul received a divine form. In a flash of light, the Gaṇas (attendants) of Śrī Śiva appeared from the sky, riding a celestial Vimāna. They picked up the purified soul and carried him away to Śivaloka the divine abode of Mahādeva. And all this happened just by the mere contact with Bhasma, not by any ritual, not by any mantras, but by the unconscious grace that flows through that sacred ash. This tale, told by Śrī Chidambara Dīkṣita Svāmī is not a myth, it is a testament to the fact that Śiva's grace does not depend on worthiness or preparation. His compassion is so vast that even an unintended association with his sacred elements becomes a cause for mokṣa.

Another story from Chidambara Caritra reveals the unimaginable compassion of Śiva through the medium of Rudrākṣa. There once lived a merchant in Nepal who sold Rudrākṣa beads for a living. Each day, he would travel to various markets with a large sack full of Rudrākṣas. To carry this weight, he relied upon his donkey, who tirelessly bore the burden of sacred beads through hills, villages, and dusty roads. The donkey never wore the Rudrākṣas, never chanted mantras, and never knew their significance. Yet, day after day, he carried thousands of Rudrākṣas on his back with silent endurance. Years passed. One day, the donkey collapsed under the load of Rudrākṣas and died. The merchant mourned the loss of his animal, but what happened next was astonishing. Attendants of Śiva descended from the sky, glowing with divine radiance. They bestowed a divine body upon the donkey's soul and carried it away to Śivaloka. The donkey, who had not consciously worshipped, was granted liberation simply because it bore the Rudrākṣa the beads formed from Śiva's own tears. This story shatters all doubts. It proves that even the creatures can attain mokṣa by associating with Śiva's sacred symbols. Śiva does not measure devotion by ritual perfection, by scriptural scholarship, or by high status. He looks for connection, however small. A single contact with Bhasma, a single moment of wearing or carrying Rudrākṣa, even if done unknowingly, can become the cause for ultimate liberation. These stories echo the truth from the Śiva Mahāpurāṇa. Śrī Śiva says, "The one who wears Bhasma or Rudrākṣa, who remembers Me even once with love, is dearer to Me than the most learned Brāhmaṇa." Such is the nature of Mahādeva, Pāśupati the Lord of all beings. He embraces all, humans and animals, sinners and saints, and gives them refuge. Just as the sun does not discriminate while giving light, Śiva does not discriminate in giving his anugraha (grace).

This universal compassion is further exemplified in the sacred temple of Śrī Kālahasti, one of the holiest Śiva temples in Bhāratavarṣa. This place is sanctified by the stories of three non-human devotees:

Śrī - The spider who offered its web to protect the Śivaliṅga

Kāla - The snake who defended the Śivaliṅga with its venom

Hasti - The elephant who brought flowers and water for worship

Each of them, driven by pure instinctive devotion, served Śiva in their own way. And in return, Śiva granted them Mokṣa, merging them into himself. Hence the name Śrī Kālahasti, where Śrī (spider), Kāla (snake), and Hasti (elephant) found eternal union with their Lord. Śiva's title Pāśupati gains deeper meaning through these stories. He is the Lord of all living beings, not just humans. He purifies whoever comes in contact with his energy, even if unconsciously.

In the journey toward Śiva, there are three sacred companions:

Nāma-japa - Chanting the holy name of Śiva, especially the pañcākṣarī mantra

Bhasma - The sacred ash that purifies and protects

Rudrākṣa - The divine beads that sanctify and stabilize the mind

These three are like the confluence of Gaṅgā, Yamunā, and Sarasvatī the Triveṇī-Saṅgama of devotion. When combined, they become a spiritual powerhouse that accelerates liberation. Just as touching the Triveṇī river brings holiness, adorning oneself with Bhasma, wearing Rudrākṣa, and chanting Śiva's name makes one pure and taintless. The glory of Bhasma and Rudrākṣa is not a matter of belief alone, it is a spiritual reality, confirmed by scriptures, saints, and stories passed through generations. From

Upaniṣadic revelations to village legends, from sages to animals, the transformative touch of Śiva manifests repeatedly.

Let these sacred symbols not remain external alone. Let them penetrate our hearts, reminding us constantly:

That the body is temporary, but the Self is eternal. That love for Śiva, even the smallest spark, is enough to set the soul free.

Bhasma reminds us that everything turns to ash, but the one who wears the ash becomes imperishable. Rudrākṣa shows that even a tear of Śiva can carry the universe within. Together, they are Śiva's grace in tangible form. Let us bow our heads to that grace, and adorn our lives with his name, his ash, and his Rudrākṣa beads.

Chapter 8

Nīlakaṇṭha Rudra

In the history of the universe, one of the most celebrated divine events is the Samudra Manthana the churning of the ocean. It was not just an act of extraction of nectar (Amṛta), but a event where the existence was tested, shaken, and ultimately redeemed by the boundless compassion of Bhagavān Śiva. It is in this very episode that the world first beheld the majestic form of Nīlakaṇṭha the blue-throated Rudra who bore the unbearable for the sake of all creation. The Devas and Asuras, ever in conflict, agreed temporarily to churn the Ocean Kṣīra Sāgara in pursuit of Amṛta the nectar of immortality. Mount Mandara was used as the churning rod, and Vāsuki the king of serpents volunteered to serve as the rope. The churning began with intensity, and a myriad of celestial treasures emerged from the depths of the ocean. The sacred cow Kāmadhenu was claimed by the ṛṣis for performing Yajñas. Airāvata the white elephant and the celestial flying horse appeared and were taken by Indra the king of the gods. Viṣṇu reclaimed his divine jewel the Kaustubha, and later welcomed Mahālakṣmī herself as she rose from the ocean, choosing Viṣṇu as her eternal consort. Yet, before the nectar could manifest, there came forth a deadly, venomous substance Hālahala. This was not an ordinary poison; it was the concentrated essence of destruction itself. Its emergence darkened the realms. Beings of Brahmaloka and Vaikuṇṭha trembled. Even Śrī Viṣṇu's form turned dark as the effects of the poison pervaded the cosmic space. The flames of Hālahala threatened to consume the worlds. Terrified and helpless, the Devas rushed to the refuge of the One who transcends fear, Bhagavān Rudra. Śiva the auspicious one whose compassion knows no bounds, appeared before them. He who resides in Kailāsa, who is untouched by gain or loss, listened to the plight of the devas with stillness. Without hesitation, without a trace of fear or pride, he took the poison in his own hands and drank it. Such was the intensity of the Hālahala that even for the great Lord, it had to be contained. At that moment, the compassionate Devī Pārvatī placed her divine hand gently on his neck, preventing the poison from traveling further into his body. The poison stayed in Śiva's throat, and his throat turned blue. Thus, he became Nīlakaṇṭha the blue-throated one. Some scriptures also revere him as Nīlakaṇṭha Mahādeva or Nīlagrīva, indicating the colour reaching up to the neck.

This act of consuming poison was not just an intervention; it was a cosmic sacrifice. Śiva did not drink it for the sake of personal glory or celestial reward. He did it for Loka-Kalyāṇa, the welfare of the worlds. It was an act of pure Karuṇā, untainted by ego or desire. This is why Śiva is called Mahādeva the Great God. He is Maheśvara, the Supreme Ruler of past, present, and future trikālagñāna personified. Even though the Devas longed for nectar to gain immortality and defeat the Asuras, it was Bhagavān Śiva's act that made that very possibility even exist. If there was no Śiva to intervene, the poison would have destroyed everything and nectar would have been meaningless.

The devas in their gratitude, sang hymns in his praise, bowing to him as the eternal, deathless one. He is Mṛtyuñjaya the conqueror of death. He is the destroyer of destruction the one whose presence neutralizes even the fiercest calamities. His body remained unaffected by the poison not because he resisted it, but because he is beyond dualities. Śiva is not just the Lord of tapas or penance; he is the source of tapas. He is Satyam, Śivam, Sundaram truth, auspiciousness, and beauty. The world praises his act as Viṣāpāna. Yet, the truth remains that only he had the capacity to hold the poison. The greatness of Śiva is such that even his reflections become worthy of worship. While the world glorifies his act of drinking the Hālahala poison, very few know about the Attendant who assisted him in this celestial sacrifice Alāla Sundarar also known as Hālahala Sundarar. In Kailāsa, where Śiva resides with Pārvatī Devī and a host of gaṇas, a unique incident occurred. One day, Śiva assumed a magnificent form the embodiment of beauty. In this form, he stood before a shining, lustrous wall in Kailāsa. The brilliance of Śiva's form was reflected upon the radiant surface. But this was no ordinary reflection. It was alive, conscious, and divine. Śiva looked at the reflection and spoke, "Emerge from the wall, O beautiful one." By the will of the Lord, the reflection separated from the wall and assumed a distinct form. This form known as Sundarar the beautiful one bowed before Śiva, ready to serve him eternally. Śiva accepted him as his attendant, a companion who would remain close and take part in divine acts. It was this Sundarar who upon receiving orders from Śiva during the

Samudra Manthana, gathered the Hālahala poison in his hands. With utmost composure and devotion, he held the terrifying venom as if it were merely a fruit. For this divine act, he became known as Hālahala Sundarar or Alāla Sundarar. The terrible poison, which could burn through worlds, lay calmly in his hands. Such was the power of his devotion and the grace he had received from Śiva. While the devas feared the poison and sought protection, this attendant of Śiva stood beside his Lord, upholding the duty of service. In doing so, he partook in one of the most pivotal moments in cosmic history. His participation is not always recounted in popular retellings, but the traditions that revere this form of Sundarar know the depth of his devotion. Later, Alāla Sundarar was born again on earth as one of the most revered Nāyanmārs, Sundaramūrti Nāyanār.

Born in Tamil lands, he came to spread the message of devotion to Śiva through his poetic hymns and deep spiritual insight. He wandered to temples, sang praises of Śiva, and awakened devotion in thousands of hearts. His compositions are still sung with reverence in temples across South India. But within him always lived the memory of his divine origin as the reflection of Śiva, as the one who held poison for his Master. Even in his earthly journey, his devotion to Śiva as Nīlakaṇṭha remained unshaken. The image of Śiva with the blue throat, bearing the mark of sacrifice was forever etched in his soul.

Ultimately, by the grace of Śiva, Sundaramūrti Nāyaṉār returned to Kailāsa reuniting with his eternal Master. He was not a mere servant; he was a manifestation of Śiva's beauty and will. Such is the leelā of

Bhagavān Śiva. In his world, even an image can attain liberation. The Pañcākṣarī mantra Namaḥ Śivāya that Sundaramūrti sang with joy, carried within it the essence of surrender. His life reminds us that to serve Śiva, to glorify the name Nīlakaṇṭha, is itself the path to Mokṣa. After Śiva consumed the terrifying Hālahala poison and retained it in his throat by the grace of Pārvatī Devī, a unique divine episode unfolded. The intense energy of the poison, though held harmlessly within Śiva's throat, revealed a tender, compassionate side of the Lord. In a lesser-known episode, Śiva, along with Pārvatī Devī, arrived in the region of Āndhra-deśa to perform a divine act that would forever in the spiritual memory of devotees. At Sūṭṭūrupalli, Śrī Śiva manifested himself in a unique form. The intensity of the cosmic act he had performed was immense, drinking the venom to save the universe. To symbolically express the repose that followed, Śiva laid his head upon the lap of Devī Pārvatī. This serene, resting form of Śiva is called Pallikondeśvara the Lord in Recline. Just as Śrī Hari Viṣṇu rests upon Ananta Śeṣa, the snake with infinite hoods, Śiva assumed a posture of divine stillness, resting on the lap of his beloved Śakti. It is crucial to understand that this act of resting was not due to weakness or discomfort, but a Leelā a divine play. As Yāśodā's scolding makes Kṛṣṇa pretend to cry, though he is all-powerful, in the same way Śiva enacted a moment of vulnerability to endear himself to devotees. The idea that he felt discomfort from the poison is symbolic. In truth, no substance in the universe can harm the one in whom the universe itself resides. Śiva is Anādi (without beginning), Ananta (without end), and Aparimita (immeasurable). He allowed this episode to happen to bless the world with the vision of Pallikondeśvara Śiva who rests not in transcendental peace. At that sacred spot, Devatās and Ṛṣis gathered. They stood with folded hands, awaiting the Lord's glance. Their hearts were filled with reverence, love, and humility. The vision of Śiva resting upon the lap of Pārvatī was unlike anything they had seen. It revealed a form of Śiva-Śakti the inseparable unity of the masculine and feminine principles, the stillness of Śiva and the grace of Śakti. The legend of Pallikondeśvara teaches that even the Supreme Being expresses love, comfort, and rest. It is not because he needs it, but because he wants to display the entire spectrum of divinity for his devotees to meditate upon. Thus, Surutupalli became sanctified as the only place where Śiva is worshipped in this reclining form.

Another divine episode that emerged from this period is the story of Śiva as Yakṣeśvara. After the devas consumed the nectar and became invincible, their gratitude toward Śiva faded. The arrogance of power, the delusion of superiority, and the illusion of independence filled their hearts. They had forgotten that their victory was made possible by the one who drank the venom, not by their own strength. To teach them humility and reveal their limitations, Śiva took a mysterious form as a Yakṣa. He appeared before the devas holding a simple blade of grass in his hand. Indra, Agni, Vāyu, and others approached the Yakṣa, curious to know who he was. The Yakṣa gently challenged them, "Try to move this blade of grass." Indra the king of gods asked Agni to burn it. The fire god tried but failed. Vāyu the wind god attempted to blow it away but could not even stir it. One by one, all their powers were rendered useless. Their pride crumbled. Then the Yakṣa disappeared. At that moment, the mother of the Universe Devī Umā (Pārvatī) appeared and revealed the truth, "It was Śiva who stood before you as the Yakṣa. He came not to challenge your strength, but to awaken your understanding." The devas bowed in shame and reverence, now truly aware of Śiva's supreme nature. This form of Śiva is known as Yakṣeśvara and the episode is a reminder that pride, even in the celestial realms, must dissolve before the presence of the Supreme. Śiva does not seek reverence, he bestows it upon those who surrender with humility. His power is silent, his actions are mysterious, and his nature is beyond all measurement. Among those deeply moved by the legend of Nīlakaṇtha was a noble devotee named Thirunīlakaṇtha. His entire being was immersed in the worship of Śrī Śiva, particularly drawn to the form of the blue-throated Lord. The mark of the blue throat symbolized to him the greatness of Śiva's sacrifice, the ultimate expression of compassion. Thirunīlakaṇtha would ceaselessly chant the name "Nīlakaṇtha, Nīlakaṇtha," letting it flow through his breath like a river of devotion. He did not care for worldly attainments or rituals. To him, the mere utterance of that sacred name was the key to all that mattered. The pañcākṣarī mantra Namaḥ Śivāya resided in his heart, but it was the divine image of the blue-throated Śiva that became his deepest meditation. Pleased by his unwavering love,

Śiva appeared before him and granted him mokṣa (liberation) from all cycles of birth and death. He was taken to Kailāsa the eternal abode where he merged with the Supreme. His life stands as a testament to the transformative power of Nāma-Smaraṇa the remembrance of the Divine Name. Thus, in this sacred chapter, we encounter not only the powerful tale of Śiva drinking poison during the Samudra Manthana, but also the hidden threads of divine wisdom:

1)Sundarar the reflection of Śiva who served him by holding the Hālahala

2)Pallikondeśvara the reclining Śiva revealing divine tenderness

3)Yakṣeśvara, the humbling force who destroyed the pride of gods

4)Thirunīlakaṇṭha the devotee who attained Kailāsa through Nāma-Bhakti.

All these forms orbit around one sacred name Nīlakaṇṭha. To chant this name is to invoke the one who saved creation, who drank the poison, who rests in stillness but acts in silence, and who dwells beyond comprehension. Even today, the name "Nīlakaṇṭha" echoes in the hearts of devotees. This is one of the prominent names of Śiva. It reminds the world about sacrifice without expectation, strength wrapped in compassion, and of the Divine whose mystery deepens the more we approach it. The legend of Nīlakaṇṭha the blue-throated Śiva unfolds during the great cosmic event known as Samudra Manthana the churning of the ocean by the devas and asuras. As treasures emerged from the ocean, a deadly poison called Hālahala surfaced, threatening to destroy the entire universe. None among the devas or asuras could withstand its potency. The worlds trembled, and even Viṣṇu's form darkened under its effect. It was then that Bhagavān Śiva the compassionate Mahādeva intervened. Without hesitation, he drank the Hālahala to save creation. To prevent the poison from spreading through his divine form, Devī Pārvatī placed her hand on his neck, keeping the venom contained in his throat. This act turned his throat deep blue, earning him the name Nīlakaṇṭha. Though Śiva remained unaffected internally, this selfless act granted the devas the opportunity to receive Amṛta and ultimately win against the asuras. Yet, in time, the devas grew arrogant, forgetting the grace that saved them. To humble them, Śiva appeared as Yakṣeśvara, a mysterious being who challenged their pride with a blade of grass. The most powerful among the devas failed to move it. Only through the guidance of Devī Umā did they realize it was Śiva who had tested them and shattered their illusion. This chapter also introduces the divine form of Pallikondeśvara where Śiva after the cosmic event, rests his head on the lap of Devī Pārvatī at Surutupalli in Andhra. Though interpreted as a sign of discomfort from the poison, this resting form is a leelā an act of grace revealing Śiva's unity with Śakti and his affection for devotees. The sight of the Lord resting surrounded by Devas and Ṛṣis becomes a source of deep devotion and reverence. Also woven into this chapter is the story of Alāla Sundarar, the reflection-born servant of Śiva. His act of holding the Hālahala in his hands is remarkable because it demonstrates the power imbued within those who are emanations of Śiva. The devas, despite their celestial might were powerless. But a reflection of Śiva born from the beauty of the Lord himself could hold destruction easily in his palms. Why? Because he did it not with fear, but with bhakti. Devotion transformed him into a vessel capable of the impossible. When he took birth again on earth as Sundaramūrti Nāyanār, the memory of that service lived in his soul. He did not wander like a sage renouncing the world. He wandered as a householder who sang with love. He composed verses that melted the hearts of even hardened men. In temples, on streets, in the presence of kings and farmers alike, he invoked the name Śiva with melody and passion. He was a lover of the Divine. There is a deep reason why Śiva chose to manifest such a being on earth. The path of

Nāma-Bhakti, the loving repetition of the Lord's name, is accessible to all. One need not be learned or austere. One only needs a longing heart, and Sundaramūrti Nāyanār became the embodiment of this path. Thus, the chapter on Nīlakaṇṭha brings together Śiva's selfless act, the devotion of his attendants, the humility he brings to the Devas, his divine rest on Devī's lap, and the eternal glory of those who chant his name with love.

Chapter 9

Śiva the Saviour

Rudra is known as the fierce one, the unapproachable by the arrogant, and the saviour of the humble-hearted. Bhagavān Rudra the terrible and compassionate is the destroyer of evil, the annihilator of adharma, and the ultimate protector of his bhaktas. His weapons are not mere tools of violence, but embodiments of divine justice. His Trident (Triśūla) pierces through illusion, ego, and ignorance, while his bow and arrows are symbols of swift divine retribution against evil. According to the ancient Vedas, Rudra is described as an archer one who wields the bow, and adorned with ash and smeared with sacred marks. The Ṛgveda (2.33.11) invokes him with both reverence and a humble plea, **"I praise you, the famous one, seated in the heart, the ever-youthful, terrible like a beast, fierce for the purpose of destruction. Rudra, having been praised by us, let your armies strike at others than us."** In this verse, the duality of Rudra's nature is beautifully captured, he is terrible to the wicked and merciful to the devotees. No force in the cosmos can withstand the impact of the arrows hurled by Rudra. Every weapon from the thunderbolt (Vajra) to the fire-arrow (Agnibāṇa) is included in his arsenal. Yet, the greatest weapon he wields is his compassion. While the devas may fight for protection and dominion, Rudra fights only when his devotees are in danger. Śiva's Triśūla is not merely a weapon, it is a symbol of the three guṇas sattva, rajas, and tamas brought under his control. When he raises it in protection of his devotees, no force of fate, karma, or death can withstand him. He is the one who stood as a wall of protection when Yama the god of death tried to claim the life of Mārkaṇḍeya a young sage and a devout worshipper of Śiva. At the age of sixteen, Mārkaṇḍeya's life was destined to end, but his unwavering devotion to Mahādeva changed the course of destiny itself. When Yama cast his noose around the boy, Mārkaṇḍeya clung to the Śivaliṅga, weeping and chanting "Oṁ Namaḥ Śivāya." That moment witnessed a divine eruption, Śrī Śiva emerged from the liṅga in a blinding form of Rudra, enraged beyond measure. He struck Yama down and granted Mārkaṇḍeya eternal youth and immortality, proclaiming that those who chant his name with love shall never fear death. Kinga Śveta also conquered death through devotion. When he surrendered his mind and desires to

Rudra, the Kāla the god of Time could not bind him. Śiva as Mahākāla appeared as Supreme Time and killed time for his devotee. Such is the power of the God of Gods (Mahādeva), who is not bound by karma but destroys its bondage for the sake of the bhakta. There is no greater protection to be sought than Śiva. He alone is the refuge. In these words, lies the core truth of Śiva-bhakti. All worldly protections wealth, might, and status fail in the face of death and suffering. But those who surrender to Śiva attain Mukti (liberation), the cessation of birth and death, and union with the divine. Human life is fleeting, and death is the unavoidable destination. After death is not a mystery for those who follow the path of dharma and devotion. If one dies with desires unfulfilled, the subtle body remains restless, wandering in liminality. The Śāstras say that such a Jīva becomes a preta (spirit). But through Śivopāsanā the worship of Śrī Śiva, even deep-seated desires dissolve like mist before the sun. It is said that desire (kāma) is the root of bondage. When there is desire, the mind becomes restless like a monkey. But when it is turned towards Mahādeva, the mind becomes free of cravings. In the heart of such a devotee, the seeds of Saṃsāra find no soil to grow. Thus, the path of devotion to Śiva is the path of freedom. By meditating on Śiva the blue-throated one, the aspirant becomes untouched by the flames of karma. As the Yogīśvara, Śiva is the knower of all paths and the revealer of the supreme knowledge. He appears in the form of Dakṣiṇāmūrti, seated under the banyan tree silently revealing Ātma-Jñāna to the Ṛṣis through mere presence. His silence speaks louder than all scriptures. One glance from him turns the most deluded into Jñānins. One touch of his grace lifts the soul beyond Māyā. Death cannot harm a true devotee of Śiva. Not because death is avoidable, but because death becomes meaningless to the one who has surrendered. The attendants of Yama, those fierce beings who drag the soul to judgment, dare not approach a Śiva-bhakta. Śiva himself walks with his devotees, burning their sins and leading them to Kailāsa the eternal abode of bliss. Such is the glory of Rudra the fierce and the merciful. He is the scorcher of death (Mṛtyumjaya) and the destroyer of sins (Pāpanāśana), and the ocean of grace (Kṛpāsindhu). Those who take refuge in him need no other protector. The glory of Śiva's compassion and his willingness to bestow Mukti upon even the most fallen is beautifully illustrated in the

Śiva Mahāpurāṇa Māhātmya, a revered section of the Skanda Mahāpurāṇa. Within its sacred verses, one finds numerous stories that highlight the unmatched grace of Mahādeva, who shields his devotees not just in life, but even in death and beyond.

One such tale is that of Devraj, a wicked Brāhmaṇa who lived a life immersed in sin, cruelty, and selfish indulgence. He never once bowed his head before dharma, and the idea of devotion never crossed his mind. He performed no tapas, no Yajña, and mocked the ways of the Sādhus. Yet, destiny took a mysterious turn at the moment of his death. As his body lay on the verge of collapse, a narrator of Purāṇic stories in Śiva temple began reciting stories from the Śiva Mahāpurāṇa. Though Devraj was not a seeker, his ears heard the sacred stories of

Śiva in his final breaths. This unintentional hearing of Mahādeva's glories became his redemption. The power of that Kathā created a surge of purity within him. When the messengers of Yama arrived to drag his soul, Śiva's gaṇas appeared with forms and weapons like fire. A battle ensued. The power of Śiva's name alone burned away the records of Devraj's sins, and he was taken to Kailāsa. He was granted Sāmīpya Mukti closeness to Śiva himself. There, he became one of the Shivagaṇas attendants of the Lord, singing his praises and living in bliss. This story is a reminder that even at the final breath, the grace of Śiva can turn around one's fate. Such is the Anugraha of Rudra. The scriptures repeat again and again, "Even the hearing of Śiva's story leads to liberation." If one listens with full faith, the burden of karma begins to melt. Smarana (remembrance), Kīrtana (glorification), and Śravaṇa (listening), these are the paths accessible to all. One need not be a scholar, ascetic, or Yogī. One must only have bhakti. Indeed, Mahādeva's compassion surpasses logic. While devas may assess merits and demerits, Śiva sees only the heart. When a person lives a life sincerely yearning for the divine, even if he stumbles on the way, Śiva lifts him. On the other hand, one who is proud of austerities but lacks humility may not find the same grace. Devotion cleanses faster than penance, for penance can inflate ego, but bhakti dissolves it. The Shāstras describe that after death, the soul faces the divine judgment. The messengers of Yama show the mirror of karma and assign the soul to Swarga or Naraka, or rebirth. But Śiva-bhaktas are spared from this chain. As stated in Liṅga Purāṇa, "The attendants of

Yama do not even come near the devotees of Śiva." To those unfamiliar with Śiva's ways, this might seem partial or unfair. But in truth, Śiva does not favour the sinner, he transforms him. That is the beauty of Śiva. He does not condemn, he redeems. He does not punish without reason, but corrects with compassion. When one turns sincerely to him, he becomes the ultimate refuge. The legend of Dakṣiṇāmūrti is another revelation of Śiva's divine mission. Seated under the banyan tree facing the south (Dakṣiṇa), the youthful Mahādeva taught the greatest knowledge not through speech, but through silence. The four ṛṣis Sanaka, Sanātana, Sanandana, and Sanatkumāra approached him with burning questions on the nature of ātman, bondage, and liberation. Śiva answered through silent transmission of truth. In that stillness, all their doubts were erased. He teaches not through intellect, but through presence. He awakens the inner knowledge already existing within the seeker. This Jñāna burns away avidyā (ignorance), much like how Śiva's third eye burns away illusion. When the inner fire of Jñāna is lit by Śiva's grace, no bondage can remain. Thus, liberation becomes effortless. Śiva's nature is unique among the Trinity. Viṣṇu preserves, Brahmā creates, but Śiva transforms. He transforms destruction into renewal, sin into merit, and fear into peace. His roles are many, as Raudra he destroys, as Śaṅkara he blesses, as Nīlakaṇṭha he swallows poison to save the cosmos, and as Bhava he gives life. The fear of death haunts every Jīva. But Śiva-bhaktas laugh at death, they know that death is not the end but a passage, a gateway into the realm of Mahādeva. One who has chanted his name, sung his praises, or meditated upon his form during life, such a soul is never lost. Śiva walks with them in their final moments. No shadow of fear dares to approach them. Śiva's connection with time (Kāla) is also noteworthy. He is called Mahākāla, greater than time itself. While Yama controls mortal death, Mahākāla governs the dissolution of the universe. At the end of a kalpa, when everything returns to the source, it is Śiva who dances the Tāṇḍava the cosmic dance of destruction. Yet, this dance is not of cruelty, but of mercy. In destruction, lies renewal. Just as the seed must break to give rise to the plant, creation must dissolve to be born a new. The Śiva Mahāpurāṇa Māhātmya repeats one eternal truth that the stories of Śiva are not mere tales, but living gateways to grace. When one listens to them, the Saṃskāras of countless births are erased.

When one reads them, the heart becomes pure. When one narrates them, others are uplifted. The power of Śiva's name, form, and Līlā is such that even if accidentally remembered, it protects.

The manifestations of Bhagavān Rudra upon Bhūloka are not mere incidents of divine play, but deeply meaningful responses to the cries of his devotees. Each place where Śiva has appeared carries a sacred vibration, and many such spots have become Kṣetras holy lands where temples stand today. Each kṣetra has its own tale. Some of these are recorded in Śāstras, while others are preserved in the hearts of local devotees, whispered from generation to generation. Every Śiva temple, especially the ancient ones, is a witness to some divine leelā some act of protection, punishment, or revelation. In each, Rudra reveals a different facet of his personality. Śiva protects his devotees. All those who dared to harm his bhaktas or disturb the sacred order of dharma met the same fate, utter annihilation. One of the most powerful narratives of Rudra's vengeance and protection is the legend of Vyāghreśvara the Lord who took down a terrible demon disguised as a tiger. This story begins after the slaying of Hiranyaksa and Hiranyakaśipu by Śrī Visnu. Though adharma had been momentarily crushed, some demonic forces still survived, driven by vengeance. Among them was a fearsome asura named Dundubhi Nirhāda. With intense hatred for the devas, he decided to disrupt their source of strength the Yajñas. In ancient times, Yajñas performed by Rsis were not only spiritual acts but also cosmic regulators. The devas drew power from these sacrifices, and in return, they sustained the world. Dundubhi Nirhāda took a cunning route. He knew he could not face the devas directly. So, he assumed the form of a tiger and began attacking ascetics and Sādhus during their rituals, particularly when they bathed in sacred rivers. In water he use to take form of dangerous animals and on land he used to take form of tiger. Several sages perished, unable to defend themselves from this monster who struck from beneath the water, unseen and unprovoked. Panic spread among the hermitages. Yajñas stopped. The sacred chants fell silent. Among these sages was one ardent devotee of Śiva who on the night of Mahāśivarātri, had just completed his Pūjā and was sitting in deep Meditation, contemplating the form of Mahādeva. That very night, Dundubhi Nirhāda taking his terrifying tiger form, crept into the temple premises. With bloodlust in his eyes, he leaped towards the devotee who remained calm, still fixed in remembrance of Śiva. In that sacred moment, when the blade of death was a breath away, Śiva appeared. Without delay, he seized the tiger in his mighty hands and struck it down with a powerful blow of his fist. The roar of Dundubhi shattered the silence of the night and echoed across the worlds. In a matter of seconds, the demonic being was dead, purified by death at the hands of Rudra.

Where this incident occurred, devotees gathered in awe and devotion. In honour of this fierce form of Śiva who destroyed the tiger demon, the Lord came to be worshipped as Vyāghreśvara the Lord of the Tiger. Even today, those the place is in

Kāśī where Śiva appeared as Vyāghreśvara. Devotees visit that sacred Kṣetra in offer prayers to him, invoking his protection from hidden enemies and seeking courage to overcome the unseen afflictions of life. The symbolism of this story is deeply spiritual. The tiger is not just an animal form. It represents the wild, unchecked forces of māyā, kāma, and krodha that attack the Sādhaka when he is close the path of realization. The river symbolizes the mind, and the emerging demon represents the Vāsanās (latent tendencies) that strike from within. When one surrenders to Śiva, he alone can strike down those inner demons. This story also reminds us of another key truth. Rudra's appearance is never without cause. When injustice prevails, when adharma dares to rise, when a devotee cries out in pain, Rudra manifests. Anger of Rudra is righteous. He may come as a sudden force, or as a subtle presence in the heart, but he comes. And when he does, he brings with him certainty that no evil shall prevail. Just as the rain falls in the rainy season and the sun rises on time every day due to the laws of cosmic order, it is out of fear of Rudra that nature continues its course. The Devatās themselves are bound to perform their roles because Rudra sustains dharma through his very existence. His mere presence upholds the balance of creation. Thus, the protection of Śiva is not a mere metaphor, it is reality. To be a Śiva-bhakta is to be wrapped in that unshakable shield. Death becomes meaningless. Suffering, though it may come, does not destroy the soul. And even the most horrific karma can be erased by a single tear shed in remembrance of Mahādeva. What then is to be feared? Śiva accepts even the fallen, lifts the weakest, and transforms the most sinful. He is not pleased by offerings of gold or grand rituals but by a sincere heart, a humble mind, and a tongue that sings his name. To read or listen to the stories of Śiva, as told in the Śiva Mahāpurāṇa Māhātmya is itself an act of worship. In each story, one finds inspiration, correction, and transformation. The tale of Devraj, the redemption of the sinful, the miracles at the time of death, all of them echo one supreme truth. Śiva is the ultimate refuge. There is no protection greater than him. He alone is the giver of Mukti. Let the world change, let death come, let karma rise, the Śiva-bhakta remains unshaken.

Chapter 10

Śiva's Supreme Mercy

Supreme Being whose presence transforms not only the hearts of men, but also the instincts of wild creatures that is Śiva the Paśupati Lord of all beings. He is not just the deity of ascetics, yogis, or sages, he is the inner soul of every living creature, the divine witness in every eye, the stillness behind every heartbeat. The divinity of Śiva is such that all beings, regardless of their nature begin to give up enmity and radiate love in his presence. Presence of Śiva uplifts and harmonizes. Whether beast or bird, herbivore or carnivore, when touched by Śiva's sacred aura, they forget hostility and begin to act out of love, wisdom, and innocence. This profound truth is echoed in the very first chapter of the Ṛibhu Gītā verse 27. There, it is said that in the presence of supreme Śiva, animals of opposite natures forget their natural enmity. The deer tends to the lion's cub with motherly affection. The cow licks the tiger's cub with love. The cat, instead of attacking, nurses the cygnet. The peahen dances joyfully to the rhythm of the serpent. All opposites dissolve into divine harmony. How remarkable it is that animals, often ruled by instinct and survival, are so deeply moved by the grace of Śiva that they choose unity over division. If such transformation is possible in creatures of instinct, what to say of human beings who consciously seek the lotus feet of Mahādeva? The mere presence of Śiva dispels fear, eradicates conflict, and opens the doors of the heart. This is not mere poetry; it is a truth realized by countless sages and saints throughout time. For Śiva is Karuṇālaya the abode of compassion. His nature is simplicity, his essence is mercy, and his grace flows not just to the pious but even to the most fallen. He is Bhola Bhaṇḍārī the innocent benefactor, who gives without measure, who responds not to elaborate rituals but to the sincerity of the heart.

Śiva's divine nature is vividly symbolized in Kailāśa, his abode. There, all contradictions coexist peacefully. Nandī the bull and vehicle of Śiva, dwells fearlessly despite Devī Pārvatī's mount being a lion a natural predator of the bull. Yet, no harm is ever done, for Śiva's presence nullifies all conflict. He is the center around which harmony naturally forms. Similarly, the serpent, which coils around Śiva's neck, is not hostile toward the mouse of Gaṇeśa or the peacock of Skanda. Ordinarily, these creatures would flee or fight one another. But in the sanctity of Śiva's presence, all creatures transcend their lower instincts. They experience peace. They live without fear. Because they are in the orbit of the Supreme Consciousness, and there, love replaces fear, wisdom replaces instinct, and silence replaces aggression. Such is the transforming power of Paśupati the Lord of all beings. He does not merely command creatures, He uplifts them. His essence awakens the Cit-śakti (power of consciousness) within every jīva. His gaze alone is enough to ignite devotion, to calm rage, and to instill bliss. This divine quality of Śiva was not only known to scriptures but also lived by great devotees like Āṉāya Nāyaṉār, who through his devotion and inner radiance, recreated this harmony amidst wild creatures. A humble cowherd by birth, he wandered through forests and fields with his cows, untouched by the noise of the world. His ornaments were simplicity, his wealth was contentment, and his crown was the Bhakti that flowed from him like a sacred river. Though he held no scriptures in his hands, his soul carried the knowledge of lifetimes, awakened through pure love for Mahādeva. His days were steeped in sadhana, milking the cows, churning curd, preparing ghee, and walking barefoot to the temple with offerings, all while his lips constantly whispered "Namaḥ Śivāya" the holy Pañcākṣarī mantra. This mantra did not just emerge from his tongue, it flowed from his entire being. In his presence, the forest transformed. The cows followed him not out of training, but because they felt safe in the company of one who was a living temple of

Śiva. And soon, not just the cows, but the entire jungle responded. Wild animals that once roamed freely with ferocity now gathered near him, drawn by the divine melodies of his flute. Āṉāya Nāyaṉār had received the Pañcākṣarī mantra dīkṣā from a sage in the forest an encounter that unlocked his inner Śiva. After that divine initiation, his life became a yajña. Every breath was mantra. Every step was pūjā. Every tune from his flute was a garland of sound offered at the feet of Śiva. As he wandered through the forest playing his flute, the very nature of wild beasts changed. Lions sat beside deer. Snakes swayed in rhythm to his music. Birds flocked together, not in fear, but in ecstatic silence. The predator and the prey rested together, immersed in the vibrations emanating from Āṉāya's soul. His music was not a mere sound, it was Nāda the pure vibration of consciousness vibrating with Śiva's name. In this way, Āṉāya did not just follow Śiva, he became a reflection of Śiva himself. His presence brought peace. His breath carried grace. His devotion radiated so strongly that it tamed the fiercest beasts, reminding them of the peace that dwells in the heart of creation. The devotee of Śiva begins to shine with the same light as his Lord. As Śiva is Paśupati, the master of beings, so too did Āṉāya become a harmonizer of beings, not through authority, but through love. This divine phenomenon mirrors what we see in Mount Kailāśa, where Śiva and Pārvatī dwell. The bull and lion co-exist. The serpent sits on Śiva's neck, yet no tension exists with the peacock of Skanda or the mouse of Gaṇeśa. There is a cosmic trust in the presence of Śiva. No creature feels threatened. The fearless purity of his being overcomes all instincts of harm. Similarly, Āṉāya's forest became a miniature Kailāśa a place where love conquered fear. This was not because Āṉāya wielded power over animals, but because he radiated the very essence of Śiva oneness, peace, and divine song. Through the Nāda of his flute and the nāma of Śiva, he tuned his entire being to the rhythm of the cosmos. Such was the power of his devotion that the jungle transformed into a temple. The trees became pillars, the birds became singers, and the animals became sages sitting at the feet of a divine musician. In the form of Āṉāya, Śiva's compassion played the flute, and the whole forest listened in silence.

Among the many paths that lead to the Divine, one of the most mysterious and deeply transformative is the path of Nāda

Yoga the union with God through sacred sound. In Nāda Yoga, sound is not merely vibration, it is consciousness itself made audible. The universe, according to ancient sages, was born from Śabda Brahman Divine Sound. And to merge with that primordial sound is to merge with the Divine source of all creation. In this sacred tradition, the mantra "Namaḥ Śivāya" is not just five syllables, it is the very essence of Śiva. It embodies the five elements (pañca mahābhūta), the five faces of Śiva, and the five currents of awareness. Chanting this mantra aligns the soul with cosmic rhythm. When music is infused with devotion and divine name, it becomes Nāda Yoga. Many saints in India have followed this sacred path. They sang not just for pleasure, but as a deep sādhana to awaken the heart, to call the Divine into their midst. Through bhajans, nāma saṅkīrtana, and mantra-japa, they tuned their souls like instruments in the hands of God. The very breath became melody, and the heart became a drumbeat of longing. One such shining example was Sant Nāmadeva, the great Varkari saint of Maharashtra, whose devotion to Viṭṭhala a form of Lord Viṣṇu, transcended ritual boundaries. Yet, his unwavering love was so pure that even Lord Śiva who resides in the sacred temple of Aundha Nāgnātha was pleased with him. Nāmadeva, traveling with fellow devotees, arrived at the ancient temple of Śiva, with the sole intent of praising Viṭṭhala through song. Unconcerned with sectarian norms, he began playing cymbals and singing bhajans in front of the temple. His music echoed with the name of Viṭṭhala, but his heart was filled with non-dual devotion, which sees no difference between Viṣṇu and Śiva. A temple priest, disturbed by what he perceived as inappropriate worship, scolded the saint, and asked him to move to the back of the temple. Simple-hearted and humble, Nāmadeva obeyed without complaint. He went to the rear of the temple and sat down under a tree, where he resumed his bhajans. So immersed did he become in the love of Viṭṭhala that he lost track of time and space. His songs were not addressed to form, but to the Supreme. Evening descended, and the temple's presiding deity, Mahādeva, stirred. Moved by the intensity of Nāmadeva's love, Śiva performed a divine act. He turned the direction of the sanctum sanctorum, so that Śiva would now face his devotee who sat singing outside the rear of the temple. This miracle was witnessed by the priest and other devotees, who realized that Śiva

Himself bows to pure bhakti. In this story lies the essence of Nāda Yoga, it is not about what is sung, but from where it is sung. When sound arises from an ego-less heart, the Divine not only listens, he moves. Whether one chants "Rāma," "Viṭṭhala," or "Śiva," if the call is true, the Divine responds. Śiva, the eternal Yogi, is known as Bhaktavatsala the lover of his devotees. He is not bound by form, ritual, or doctrine. He listens not just to the words, but to the bhāva behind them. The flute of Āṉāya Nāyaṉār and the cymbals of Nāmadeva both struck the same chord in the heart of Śiva the note of pure devotion. In Nāda Yoga, it is not necessary to renounce the world or wear ochre robes. What is required is surrender, sincerity, and sacred sound. When the name of God becomes your breath, your song, your heartbeat, then God becomes your listener, your companion, and your Self.

The Divine listens not only with ears, but with presence. And in that sacred silence between the notes, Śiva reveals Himself. The names of Śiva are not just titles or poetic epithets, they are doorways into divine realization. Each name carries a vibration, a facet of the Supreme, and to chant these names is to invoke the very qualities they represent. Āṉāya Nāyaṉār, through his loving remembrance and constant chanting, invoked many of these sacred names. His being resonated with their meanings, and his soul became an embodiment of those divine attributes. Let us explore some of these names, as the sages have explained them, each one a jewel.

Śiva : The word Śiva means auspicious, pure, and benevolent. He is the embodiment of śānti (peace), untouched by impurity or malice. To chant "Śiva" is to align with well-being and spiritual purity. It is the vibration of the one who brings welfare to all.

Śaṅkara : Śaṅkara means the giver of happiness. He bestows ānanda, the bliss that arises from surrender and liberation. Devotees find inner joy in simply remembering him, for he gives joy without asking anything in return.

Gaurīśa : As the consort of Gaurī (another name of Pārvatī), Śiva is called Gaurīśa the Lord of Gaurī. This name expresses the union of Śiva and Śakti.

Nīlakaṇṭha : This name means "Blue-Throated One", referring to the episode during the ocean churning when Śiva drank the deadly kālakūṭa poison to save the cosmos. Instead of swallowing it, he held it in his throat. His blue throat reminds us of sacrifice for the good of all beings, a symbol of infinite compassion.

Trilocana : Trilocana means "the Three-Eyed One". His third eye signifies Jñāna (wisdom), Icchā (will), and Kriyā (action). These eyes also represent the sun, moon, and fire. With his third eye, he burned Kāmadeva the god of desire, teaching that true bliss lies beyond the senses. Alternate names with similar meaning: Trayambaka, Trayākṣa, Vīrūpākṣa.

Maheśvara : A combination of Maha (great) and Īśvara (lord), this name means "The Great Lord", the Supreme Ruler who governs all gods and universes. Maheśvara is not bound by any single realm, he pervades all.

Mahādeva : Similar in meaning to Maheśvara, Mahādeva means "The God of Gods". Merely chanting this name three times is said to draw Śiva's gaze and blessings. "Mahādeva, Mahādeva, Mahādeva" is a call that melts even the silence of the mountains.

Tripurāntaka : This name means "Destroyer of the Three Cities", referring to the episode where Śiva destroyed the three demonic cities (Tripura) with a single arrow. It signifies the destruction of ego, illusion, and ignorance. Similar names: Tripurāri, Purāri, Puraśāsana.

Dhurjati : Śiva is called Dhurjati because he holds the Gaṅgā in his matted hair. This name, meaning "one with matted locks", symbolizes control of the senses and the sacred connection between earth and the heavens. Other names: Kapardin, Jaṭil.

Kālaśāsana : This means "Conqueror of Time". He is Kālātīta beyond the past, present, and future. Time cannot touch him. He is the eternal stillness in which all movement appears. He is also Mahākāla the great Time itself, and its dissolution.

Kāmārī - The enemy of the god of desire Kāma. Śiva destroyed desire with his third eye, showing that liberation lies beyond attachment. One who meditates on this name gains strength over inner lust and passions.

Kālakāṇṭha - Another form of Nīlakaṇṭha, this name also refers to the one who drank poison. It emphasizes Śiva's fearless acceptance of suffering for the sake of others. The poison rests in his throat, but it does not affect him, symbolizing supreme control over negativity.

Kāladhara - Bearer of the crescent moon. The moon upon Śiva's head represents coolness of mind, serenity, and the cycle of time. He wears time like an ornament, never controlled by it.

Karuṇālaya - The abode of compassion. Śiva, though fierce in form, is tender in heart. He blesses even the outcast, the broken, the impure. His gaze sees the soul, not the skin.

Each name that Āṉāya chanted was not just a sound, it was a flame of awareness. These names shaped his consciousness, elevated his being, and invited the presence of Śiva to dwell within him. He did not need complex rituals, his breath, his flute, his song, and his heart were enough. To chant the names of Śiva with love is to walk the path of liberation.

Here we conclude the Book **MELODY OF SHIVA PANCHAKSHARI.** Thanks

Namah Shivaya

Suggestions are welcome on Instagram

Contact @maha_shiva_ for any queries or suggestions related to Book